# Don't Call Me Gentle Charles!

An Essay on Lamb's *Essays of Elia*

by

Robert Frank

D0736279

Corvallis: Oregon State University Press

**Library of Congress Cataloging in Publication Data**

Frank, Robert, 1939-
   Don't call me gentle Charles!

   (Studies in literature; 2) (Oregon State monographs)
   Bibliography: pp. 137-140
   Includes index.
     1. Lamb, Charles, 1775-1834. Essays of Elia.
I. Title.  II. Series: Studies in literature
(Corvallis, Or.); 2.
PR4861.F7       824'.7       75-34318
ISBN 0-87071-082-6

DON'T CALL ME GENTLE CHARLES!

OREGON STATE MONOGRAPHS
STUDIES IN LITERATURE

Walter C. Foreman, *Consulting Editor*

# ACKNOWLEDGMENT

Friends and colleagues have been kind enough to read and criticize various sections of this book. For their constructive suggestions and encouragement I express my gratitude to Jesse Bone, Walter Foreman, Chester Garrison, Eric Gould, Hoover W. Jordan, and Thomas V. Moore. I am especially happy to express my thanks for his advice and many kindnesses to James Scoggins, in whose seminar this study first took shape, and who offered constant encouragement during the writing of it. I am also grateful to Kathryn Moore, Dia Shuhart, and Sharon Springer for helping me prepare the manuscript.

Neither praise nor thanks can express my debt to my wife, Arva, for her patience, understanding, and unfailing support.

# TABLE OF CONTENTS

M Y GENTLE-HEARTED CHARLES! when the last rook
     Beat its straight path along the dusky air
Homewards, I blest it! deeming its black wing
(Now a dim speck, now vanishing in light)
Had cross'd the mightly Orb's dilated glory,
While thou stood'st gazing; or, when all was still,
Flew creeking o'er thy head, and had a charm
For thee, my gentle-hearted Charles, to whom
No sound is dissonant which tells of Life.

S. T. COLERIDGE in "This Lime-Tree Bower My Prison"


"In the next edition of the 'Anthology' . . . please to blot
out *gentle-hearted,* and substitute: drunken dog, ragged-head,
seld-shaven, odd-eyed, stuttering, or any other epithet which
truly and properly belongs to the gentleman in question."

CHARLES LAMB to S. T. COLERIDGE, August 14, 1800

# INTRODUCTION

A REVIEW of scholarly and critical studies of Charles Lamb
reveals that most of the books and articles about him
have been concerned first with his life and last with his writings.[1] E. V. Lucas, his biographer, regards the life of Lamb as
"the narrative of one who was a man and brother first, an
East India clerk next, and a writer afterwards."[2] Lucas' remarks are both descriptive and evaluative. Lamb's story, he
continues, is that of a "private individual who chanced to
have literary genius" rather than "of a man of letters in the
ordinary sense of the term. The work of Charles Lamb forms
no integral part of the history of English literature: he is not
in the main current, he is hardly in the side current of the
great stream."[3] Lamb did not devote most of his life to writing, but to conclude that he is outside the mainstream of
English literature on that basis is unfair to Lamb and to the
essays.

Even more recent students of Lamb, who state that they
recognize his merits as a writer, appear reluctant to claim too
much for the essays. George L. Barnett echoes Lucas' judgment: "Lamb was not a professional author, writing for other

---

[1] For an excellent discussion of the studies on Lamb see George
L. Barnett and Stuart M. Tave, "Charles Lamb," in *The English Romantic Poets and Essayists: A Review of Research and Criticism,* rev.
ed., ed. Carolyn W. Houtchens and L. H. Houtchens (New York:
New York University Press, 1966), pp. 37-74.

[2] E. V. Lucas, *The Life of Charles Lamb,* 4th rev. ed. (London:
Methuen, 1921), II, 546.

[3] Lucas, p. 547.

authors, but a working man writing for the average reader—
of his own day, or today."[4] I would not argue with the intelligence or taste of the average reader, but with the assump-
tion that Lamb did not aim higher, as for example, did
Wordsworth or Coleridge.

Only in the last few years have the excellence of Lamb's
essays and their position in the romantic movement received
attention. Fundamental to the discussions of Richard Haven,
Donald Reiman, and Daniel Mulcahy is the belief that
Lamb's achievement is noteworthy and in the mainstream of
romantic literature.[5] Haven argues that Lamb is doing in
prose "something akin to what others, especially Wordsworth and Coleridge, were doing in poetry, and his essays
at their best exhibit an equally careful and artful poetic
structure."[6] Lamb brought to his essays a concern for crafts-
manship that had generally been reserved for poetry.

Through examining the essays of Elia—seven in detail—
I hope to show that they will bear the kind of critical atten-
tion that has been given the poetry of the romantic period.
The seven essays considered in detail are: "Blakesmoor in
H---shire," "The Old Benchers of the Inner Temple," "Mrs.
Battle's Opinions on Whist," "Mackery End, in Hertford-
shire," "The Superannuated Man," "New Year's Eve," and
"Old China."

---

[4] *Charles Lamb: The Evolution of Elia* (Bloomington, Ind.:
Indiana Univ. Press, 1964), p. 5.

[5] "The Romantic Art of Charles Lamb," *ELH*, 30 (1963), 137-
46; "Thematic Unity in Lamb's Familiar Essays," *JEGP*, 64 (1965),
470-78; "Charles Lamb: The Antithetical Manner and the Two
Planes," *SEL*, 3 (1963), 517-42. I have tried to acknowledge specific
debts in the notes, but I am most indebted to these three discussions
for suggesting the many riches of the *Essays of Elia*.

[6] "The Romantic Art . . .," p. 137.

# I

## THE CREATION OF A NEUTRAL WORLD

No less than Wordsworth or Coleridge, Lamb was well aware of the difficulties posed for a serious writer of literature by a public that failed to distinguish between an aesthetic experience and other modes of consciousness—ethical, practical, or critical. He faced the problem of educating a public so that it would respond sympathetically and imaginatively to his *Essays of Elia:* he wanted the essays to be treated as art objects, not as the scribblings of a journalist. Lamb had first-hand knowledge of the tastes and critical habits of the London public. A playgoer, he observed the actions of many audiences at the theater. In the essay "On the Artificial Comedy of the Last Century," Elia attributes the extinction of the comedy of manners during his time to the expectations brought to the plays by an audience spoiled by the

exclusive and all devouring drama of common life; where the
moral point is every thing; where, instead of the fictitious half-
believed personages of the stage (the phantoms of old comedy)
we recognize ourselves, our brothers, aunts, kinsfolk, allies,
patrons, enemies,—the same as in life,—with an interest in what
is going on so hearty and substantial, that we cannot afford our
moral judgment, in its deepest and most vital results, to compromise or slumber for a moment. What is *there* transacting, by no
modification is made to affect us in any other manner than the
same events or characters would do in our relationships of life.[1]

Elia regrets the disappearance of "all that neutral
ground of character, which stood between vice and virtue;
or which in fact was indifferent to neither, where neither
properly was called in question" (II, 142). Although restricted to Restoration Comedy, these comments by Elia
provide valuable clues to some of Lamb's designs in the
essays attributed to Elia. Lamb, I believe, wanted to create
a "neutral ground" in these essays, "a world with no med-
dling restrictions," where he and his readers, free from a
critical spirit, could breathe "imaginary freedom" beyond
the confines of "strict conscience" (II, 142).

Lamb's opinions about the tastes of the London public
and his feelings about the nature of art are not restricted to
this essay of Elia. Similar statements are found throughout
Lamb's letters, in the essays, and especially in his work
prior to the *Essays of Elia.* He held the press primarily responsible for fostering in the public a critical spirit that prevented an unfettered enjoyment of reading. In the second
Lepus paper, "Readers Against the Grain," Lepus decries
the voracious appetite of the monstrous periodical press:

---

[1] *The Works of Charles and Mary Lamb,* ed. E. V. Lucas (London: Methuen, 1903-5), II, 142. Volume number and page numbers
for subsequent quotations from the *Works* will be given in the text.

How it gapes and takes in its prescribed diet, as little savoury as
that which Daniel ministered to that Apocryphal dragon, and
not more wholesome! Is there no stopping the eternal wheels of
the Press for a half century or two, till the nation recover its
senses? Must we *magazine* it and *review* [it] at this sickening rate
for ever? Shall we never again read to be *amused?* but to judge,
to criticise, to talk about it and about it?

(I, 274)

Theatergoers are also, as we have seen, the objects of
Lamb's observations and remarks. In a discussion of the
audiences with which he was familiar at the Drury Lane
Theater, Lamb writes:

In the pit first begins that accursed critical faculty, which, making
a man the judge of his own pleasures, too often constitutes him
the executioner of his own and others! You may see the *jealousy
of being unduly pleased,* the *suspicion of being taken in to ad-
mire;* in short, the vile critical spirit, creeping and diffusing itself,
and spreading from the wrinkled brows and cloudy eyes of the
front row sages and newspaper reporters (its proper residence),
till it infects and clouds over the thoughtless, vacant countenance,
of John Bull tradesmen, and clerks of counting houses, who, but
for that approximation, would have been contented to have
grinned without rule, and to have been pleased without asking
why.

(I, 159)

Lamb exaggerated the thoughtless appearance of the
clerks and tradesmen to make his point. He was not asking
for a mindless public, rather for an audience that enjoyed a
performance without bringing to it a great many moral preconceptions and critical expectations.

Of constant interest to Lamb in his essays devoted to
the drama are the conventions of the theater, particularly
the manner in which they operate to create a sense of illusion. A skillful actor, Lamb writes, "by seeming to engage
*our* compassion for the insecure tenure" (II, 164) by which

a miser holds his money disarms his character of a great deal of its odiousness. The miser becomes sympathetic, and "a diverting likeness is substituted for a very disagreeable reality" (II, 164). Stage business creates a bond of understanding between the audience and the actors. An audience's pleasure arises from its awareness that the hateful actions of misers and the pitiable infirmities of old age are being *acted* before it. These actions "please by being done under the life, or beside it; not *to the life*" (II, 164).

The problem, however, as Lamb saw it, was that the will to judge illusion as reality was depriving playgoers of a true aesthetic experience. Audiences failed to distinguish between an illusion of reality and reality itself, demanding of the former that it faithfully mirror common life. Lamb knew, then, that the success of his *Essays of Elia* depended to a great extent on his ability to blunt and frustrate the expectations of readers who would come to the essays to sharpen their moral and critical faculties. And so Lamb carefully and unobtrusively created a context for the essays that would disarm and for the moment put to sleep these faculties of his readers. They were asked to suspend their judgment and their sense of disbelief.

In their introduction to a recent collection of essays titled *The Art of Victorian Prose*, George Levine and William Madden make a remark that is applicable to Lamb's method in the essays: "The importance of context is evident in the frame of the theatrical stage, which serves to make any response but applause, or controlled feeling inappropriate, even to dramas about murder."[2] Like dramatists, Lamb took care to create a context that would elicit an appropriate re-

---

[2] (London: Oxford Univ. Press, 1968), p. xii.

sponse. By the character of Elia, the choice of the unpretentious essay form, and the selection of unassuming objects
and trivial subjects, Lamb created a context for the essays,
similar in its effects to the conventions of the stage. The context of the essays signaled their separation from the real
world. The reader is in effect obliquely asked to put aside
his preconceptions and to prepare himself for a new type of
experience, beginning in delight and ending in a liberation
of consciousness.

Lamb would have as his readers men and women who
are as imaginatively responsive to his essays as he was to
Renaissance drama, or to the prose of Jeremy Taylor and Sir
Thomas Browne. The unassuming character in the person of
Elia, the essay form, and the preference for humble materials also served Lamb in his deliberate efforts to avoid egotism; he applied these details of his art to the solution of
problems created by the use of the subjective voice.

At the center of Lamb's rhetorical method is the creation of Elia. To write a series of essays under a fictitious
name was not new in the essay tradition. Lamb knew well
Elia's predecessors, creations such as Isaac Bickerstaff, Roger
DeCoverly, Adam Fitz-Adam, and Lien Chi Altangi. He had
read the periodical essayists. "The *Spectator* I liked extremely," he writes, "but the *Tatler* took my fancy most. I
read the others soon after, the *Rambler,* the *Adventurer,* the
*World,* the *Connoisseur.*"[3] Lamb served his apprenticeship
under the Addisonian convention. Like the earlier periodical
essayists, he signed some of his essays with names reflecting

---

[3] Quoted by George L. Barnett, *Charles Lamb: The Evolution of
Elia* (Bloomington, Ind.: The Indiana Univ. Press, 1964), p. 43.

the nature of the subjects under discussion: "Crito," "Mori-
turus," "Edax," and "Pensilis." But the attribution of the essays to Elia is different from the use of names like Crito or
even pseudonyms like Isaac Bickerstaff.

What is unique is Lamb's creation of a full personality
for Elia. Elia is his most famous character. Lamb's account
of the origin of the name Elia and the reasons for his choice
of a pseudonym have generally been accepted at face value.
He took the name, he tells us, from an old Italian clerk who
was at the South-Sea House during his time there, 1791-1792,
the months between his leaving Christ's Hospital and his
going to work at the East India House. In a letter to John
Taylor, editor of the *London Magazine*, Lamb, referring to
the South-Sea House essay, explains his reason for using Elia:
"I having a brother now there, and doubting how he might
relish certain descriptions in it, I clapt down the name of
Elia to it, which passed off pretty well, for Elia himself added
the function of an author to that of a scrivener, like myself."[4] The similarities of Elia's situation to his own and his
regard for the feelings of his brother seem a simple enough
explanation for the use of the name Elia. But it seems very
unlikely that Lamb, who paid such careful attention to all
the details of his essays, and whose comments on the periodical essayists show his familiarity with the conventions of the
form, would have created Elia solely out of deference to his
brother's feelings. It is more plausible that Lamb realized the
many advantages of such a choice as he began to write a
series of essays.

---

[4] *The Letters of Charles Lamb: To Which Are Added Those of
His Sister Mary* (hereafter cited as *Letters*), ed. E. V. Lucas (London:
J. H. Dent; Methuen, 1935), II, 302.

Lamb concluded that the success of a series of essays depended to a great degree on the color and unity given it by a strong personality. In a yet unpublished review of the first volume of Hazlitt's *Table Talk*, Lamb points to the autobiographical quality as the unifying force of the essays. He begins the review with this general observation:

A series of Miscellaneous Essays, however well executed in the parts, if it have not some pervading character to give a unity to it, is ordinarily as tormenting to get through as a set of aphorisms, or a jest-book.—The fathers of Essaywriting in ancient and modern times—Plutarch in a measure, and Montaigne without mercy or measure—imparted their own personal peculiarities to their themes. By this balm are they preserved.[5]

That Lamb's estimate of the success of the earlier essayists was just is evident from the continuous interest in Elia. Both the friends and enemies of Elia have been more interested in his personality than in his work. But the interest in Elia does not satisfactorily account for the creation of the character of Elia, since Lamb could have used his own name, as Montaigne did, and projected his own personality in the essays.

Lamb emphasizes certain qualities in Elia's character, and it is these traits that he wants us to notice on first reading an essay, since they partially determine our reaction to it. He presents Elia as a somewhat eccentric valetudinarian, who is honest and whimsical, with an amiable disposition and a spirit of self-denial. Addison and Steele employed a fictitious mouthpiece who was characterized by his omniscience; he had the knowledge of one intimately acquainted with all of London life, its men and women, their fashionable ideas,

---

[5] Quoted by Barnett, p. 43.

their tastes and opinions. Elia, however, is notable for his professed limitations of character and knowledge. He repeatedly refers to his unimportance. He professes to know little about history and chronology. Of geography he has less knowledge than a very young schoolboy. "In everything that relates to *science*, I am a whole Encyclopedia behind the rest of the world" (II, 49), he admits. He depreciates his own activities and defers quite often to the opinions of another. He admits a total lack of appreciation of any music beyond the simplest ballad tune and a lack of any "skill in figuring" (II, 2). He disagrees with old Sarah Battle's opinion on cards, "with great deference to the old lady's judgment on these matters" (II, 37).

He appears as an ineffectual presence in the daily affairs of men. "Odd, out of the way, old English plays, and treatises, have supplied me with most of my notions, and ways of feeling" (II, 49), Elia writes. "Shy of novelties" (II, 27), he prefers to dwell on pleasant memories of the past and to indulge his fancies. In the "Preface, by a Friend of the Late Elia" to the *Last Essays of Elia,* Lamb confirms the opinion of those who see Elia as childlike, even childish. Elia, he writes, "did not conform to the march of time, but was dragged along in the procession. His manners lagged behind his years. He was too much of the boy-man. The *toga virilis* never sate gracefully on his shoulders" (II, 153).

A sense of vulnerability and a vague desire for protection are other qualities constant in the character of Elia. His life is a move from one enclosure to another.[6] He was born

---

[6] F. V. Morley, *Lamb before Elia* (London: Jonathan Cape, 1932), sees Elia as the culmination of a series of dodges by Lamb to escape from love, friendship, and finally life. Lamb, she believes, escapes from the world behind the mask of renunciation, Elia.

in the Inner Temple, went to Christ's, vacationed at Blakes-moor, and worked at the South Sea House. Most comfortable in enclosed places, whether gardens or buildings, he loves to spend his vacations at Oxford and to pretend that he is a scholar in some quiet nook on campus. He seeks respite from the cares of the world in memories of childhood. He drinks in the profound peace and silence at a Quakers' meeting and delights in the recluse pleasures of a convalescent. A trifler, he would like to spend good parts of his day whiling away the hours at cards with his cousin Bridget.

Elia's confessions of diffidence and ignorance have been, unfortunately, read as autobiographical admittances of Charles Lamb. Lamb the comforting angel, the solacer of men's cares, and the flatterer of their own inadequacies and foibles is well known to readers of discussions on Lamb. Denys Thompson, who is probably the most virulent of Lamb's critics, is astonished that Lamb should still be read. He compares him with Addison only to illustrate Lamb's shortcomings. Lamb's mind is regressive, "shrinking from full consciousness."[7] His personality is fake and his style is artificial. But Thompson singles out for his harshest criticism what he considers Lamb's catering to the *l'homme sensual moyen*, flattering him into accepting his ignorance and weakness. Mario Praz damns with faint praise. He finds the reason for Lamb's rise to popularity in his ability to express "the quintessence of the bourgeois soul."[8] Praz, Thompson, and even many good friends of Elia have, I believe, been gulled by Lamb. They describe qualities in the character of Elia

[7] "Our Debt to Lamb," in *Determinations*, ed. F. R. Leavis (London: Chatto & Windus, 1934), p. 205.

[8] "The Letters of Charles Lamb or Religio Burgensis," *English Studies*, 18 (1936), p. 19.

and attribute them to Lamb without distinguishing between
Elia and his creator. They fall victim to Lamb's pretenses
without understanding their significance.

Edmund Blunden, a sympathetic student of Lamb and
his essays for many years, recognized and commented on
this characterization of Lamb as an amiable eccentric:

> Lamb is frequently fobbed off as a contemporary of Wordsworth
> and of Keats who liked roast pig, puns, dogs'-eared books, whist,
> artificial language, writing for magazines, quotations and par-
> odies; who disliked churches, Goethe, the Lake District, philoso-
> phy, punctuality, Shelley's voice, sanity, Scots, Jews and school-
> masters. If it is so, it is not surprising; for nobody has been more
> ingenious in professing unimportance than Lamb, except Lear's
> Fool.[9]

A man, in short, whose likes and dislikes showed his
lack of intelligence, taste, and wit. To read Elia as a disguised
Charles Lamb is to be unaware of a number of facts of
Lamb's life and too dependent on the essays for an estimate
of the man. To argue that there are not similarities would be
as foolish and misrepresentative as to see Elia as an older
Lamb, but it is necessary to remember that Elia is a deliberate creation, in many significant ways unlike Lamb, if we
are to read the essays intelligently. It is beyond the limits of
this study to discuss in any detail the differences between
Elia and Lamb, and yet several observations about the life
and character of Lamb should be made before I return to
Elia.

Elia's preference for old plays and treatises, for example, leaves us with the image of a wizened antiquarian, hud-
dled over his books. However, B. W. Procter speaks of

---

[9] *Charles Lamb and His Contemporaries* (Hamden: Archon
Books, 1967), p. 4.

Lamb's knowledge of old English literature and adds: "He had more knowledge of old English literature than any man whom I ever knew. He was not an antiquarian. He neither hunted after commas, nor scribbled notes which confounded his text."[10] Elia too gives the impression that he did little reading beyond the writers of the seventeenth century. But George L. Barnett writes: "It is startling to discover that there are more quotations in his [Lamb's] essays from parts of the eighteenth century than there are from those of the fifteenth, sixteenth, and seventeenth centuries put together, still excluding the drama."[11] There are also quotations in the essays from Wordsworth, Coleridge, Landor, Leigh Hunt, Procter, and Thomas Moore.

Nor was Lamb as reticent and spiritless as the character of Elia would lead us to think, or as Thompson and others argue that he was. Lamb's epigrams against the Regent, his visits to the Hunts while they were imprisoned, his defense, in an open letter, of Leigh Hunt against Southey who publicly rebuked Hunt for his lack of Christian faith, and his censure in a published leter in 1825 of the Unitarians for accepting the privileges of the Established Church of which they disapproved—all these actions show that Lamb could speak out and act when occasion called.

Lamb was the close friend of many of the writers of his time and the respected acquaintance of many other men of wit and talent. Their letters, journals, and recorded remarks include many warm references to Lamb's genius and charac-

---

[10] *Charles Lamb: His Life Recorded by His Contemporaries* (London: L. & Virginia Woolf, 1934), p. 221. (Hereafter cited as Blunden). This compilation of references to Lamb by his contemporaries is a valuable aid to students of Lamb.

[11] Barnett, p. 224.

ter. Eliza Cook's *Journal* for the year 1831 includes an account of her and her husband's last interview with Lamb at
Enfield. She describes their reception and adds: "As soon as
we were seated we saw that we were in the presence of a su-
perior man—a man of cultivated, powerful, and original
mind."[12] Her observations have the frequent support of her
contemporaries, but what is noteworthy about her remarks is
that this visit with Lamb was made just a few years before
his death in 1834, at a time when, if we are to believe Car-
lyle's record of his visit to Lamb, Lamb was little short of a
driveling idiot. There is finally the judgment of his lifelong
friend Coleridge:

> Charles Lamb has more totality and individuality of character
> than any other man I know, or have ever known in all my life. In
> most men we distinguish between the different powers of their
> intellect as one being predominant over the other. The genius
> of Wordsworth is greater than his talent though considerable. The
> talent of Southey is greater than his genius though respectable;
> and so on. But in Charles Lamb it is altogether one; his genius is
> talent, and his talent is genius, and his heart is as whole and one
> as his head.[13]

These evidences of Lamb's genius and character are
far from conclusive, but they should support my contention
that Lamb was deliberately creating a certain type of character in Elia for several related reasons.

Elia's modesty and unassuming manner gain our confidence. His frequent expressions of diffidence and confessions
of ignorance suggest to us that what Elia has to say is probably not very important or noteworthy. From Elia's manner
and his tone the reader determines that the essays are not a

---

[12] Blunden, p. 190.
[13] Blunden, p. 247.

close criticism of events or a reasoned exposition of theories and ideas. And so he relaxes his moral and critical faculties and approaches the essays as if they were to be read for sport. Lamb's reader is to be similar to the "*genuine spectator* . . . a shopkeeper and his family, whose honest titillations of mirth, and generous chucklings of applause, cannot wait or be at leisure to take the cue from the sour judging faces about them" (I, 159). Lamb hoped that the reader's pleasure would remain and accompany him in a deeper aesthetic experience of the essays.

Thomas Hood, in his recollection of visits to Lamb, describes the sort of spirit that Lamb was trying to suggest by the unassuming character of Elia. Hood has pleasant memories of "extempore assemblies at Colebrook Cottage. It was wholesome for the soul but to breathe its atmosphere. It was a House of Call for All Denominations. Sides were lost in that circle, men of all parties postponed their partisanship, and met as on a neutral ground."[14] It is exactly this same sort of "neutral ground" that Lamb wanted to establish in his essays, where taking sides and having opinions was not necessary. Since he could not actually relate the essays, he wrote a controlling presence into them. That Lamb succeeded with some of his readers is evident from Leigh Hunt's description of his experience with the essays.

In the *Examiner* Hunt refers to an anticritical spirit in Lamb's productions that "tends so much to reconcile us to all that is in the world, that the effect is almost neutralizing to every thing but complacency and a quiet admiration."[15] Hunt is describing the process whereby Lamb suggests that

---

[14] Blunden, p. 124.
[15] Blunden, p. 81.

we suspend our sense of disapprobation. In the same passage, Hunt also comments on the results of mistaken readings of Lamb's rhetorical method. A reviewer, he writes, "mistook the exquisite simplicity and apprehensiveness of Mr. Lamb's genius for want of power; and went vainly brushing away at some of the solidest things in his work under the notion of its being chaff."[16]

The characterization of Elia as a reticent man, affecting to know very little, is also Lamb's solution to some of the problems raised by the use of the subjective voice. The adoption of the forms of autobiography, reminiscence, confession, and the lyric posed difficulties for the romantics. By attributing the essays to someone who is humble, amiable, and frank, Lamb could avoid many of the difficulties accompanying the expression of the romantic ego. "I have sickened on the modern rhodomontade & Byronism, and your plain Quakerish Beauty has captivated me,"[17] he writes to Bernard Barton.

Lamb personally experienced the pride and the egos of his contemporaries a number of times. Coleridge was a lifelong friend and often saw Lamb in London. E. V. Lucas recounts the story of Lamb's reply to Coleridge's question, " 'Charles, did you ever hear me preach?' "—" 'I never heard you do anything else.' "[18] Lamb also experienced the sober anger of William Wordsworth on several occasions. In a letter to Thomas Manning, he relates the results of remarks that he had made in a recent letter to Wordsworth about the second volume of the *Lyrical Ballads*. In his letter to Words-

---

[16] *Ibid.*

[17] *Letters*, II, 332.

[18] *The Life of Charles Lamb*, 5th rev. ed. (London: Methuen, 1921), II, 822. (Hereafter cited as *Life.*)

worth, he had enumerated several of the passages that had most moved him:

adding, unfortunately, that [he writes to Manning] no single piece had moved me so forcibly as the *Ancient Mariner, The Mad Mother,* or the *Lines at Tintern Abbey.* The Post did not sleep a moment. I received almost instanteously a long letter of four sweating pages from my Reluctant Letter-Writer, the purport of which was, that he was sorry his 2d vol. had not given me more pleasure (Devil a hint did I give that it had *not pleased me*), and 'was compelled to wish that my range of sensibility was more extended, being obliged to believe that I should receive large influxes of happiness and happy Thoughts' (I suppose from the L.B.).[19]

Lamb would have appreciated Keats's impatience (expressed in a letter to John Hamilton Reynolds) with some of the qualities in the works of his contemporaries: "It may be said that we ought to read our Contemporaries—that Wordsworth, etc., should have their due from us. But, for the sake of a few fine imaginative or domestic passages, are we to be bullied into a certain Philosophy, engendered in the whims of an Egotist."[20]

Lamb early recognized his own tendency toward self-dramatization and an impulse to confess all. After having described to Coleridge his complex emotional state, experienced while eating with some friends two days after the tragic death of his mother, Lamb adds: "I mention these things because I hate concealment, and love to give a faithful journal of what passes within me."[21]

Lamb's critical abilities were perceptive enough that he did not have to rely on the judgment of reviewers for his

---

[19] *Letters,* I, 246.

[20] *The Letters of John Keats 1814-1821,* ed. Hyder E. Rollins (Cambridge, Mass.: Harvard Univ. Press, 1958), I, 223.

[21] *Letters,* I, 44.

opinions about the weaknesses of contemporary poetry, yet he was undoubtedly influenced, when he wrote the essays, by the criticism in the *Blackwood's Magazine* and the *Edinburgh Review* of the faults of the Lake School and the Cockneys. Francis Jeffrey of the *Edinburgh* criticized Byron's posturings, Leigh Hunt's affectations, and Wordsworth's egotism. By attributing his work to Elia, a deliberately created anti-hero, Lamb hoped to prevent similar charges being made against him. Leigh Hunt recognized the qualities of Lamb's genius and saw Lamb as a possible corrective to the faults of the Lake Poets. Lamb had, he writes, "a more real tact of humanity, a modester, Shakespearean wisdom, than any of them; and had he written more, might have delivered the school victorious from all its defects."[22]

Furthermore, Elia could be used to obviate any personal criticism that might be made of the writer of the essays. In "New Year's Eve," Lamb briefly drops the character of Elia and addresses us: "If these speculations seem fantastical to thee, reader—(a busy man, perchance), if I tread out of the way of thy sympathy, and am singularly-conceited only, I retire, impenetrable to ridicule, under the phantom cloud of Elia" (II, 29). Many readers of the essays did, in fact, consider them true accounts of Lamb's own experiences. The essay "Confessions of a Drunkard," included in the *Last Essays of Elia*, the Second Edition of 1835, first appeared in a quarterly magazine entitled *The Philanthropist* in 1813, and later in a revised form in the *London Magazine*, August 1822, as one of the Elia essays. A reviewer in the *Quarterly Review*, April 1822, of Reid's *Essays on Hypochondriasis and other Nervous Affections*, in a passage introducing quotations from Lamb's

---

[22] Edmund Blunden, *Leigh Hunt's "Examiner" Examined 1808-1825* (London: Cobden-Sanderson, 1928), p. 131.

essay, says: "In a collection of tracts 'On the Effects of Spirituous Liquors,' by an eminent living barrister, there is a paper entitled the 'Confessions of a Drunkard,' which affords a fearful picture of the consequences of intemperance, and which we have reason to know is a true tale."[23] Whether the tale was true or not is unimportant; what is pertinent is that Lamb, because of the subjective nature of his materials, would have to be wary of having his fiction construed as fact. Lamb probably had this review in mind when he wrote his "Preface, by a Friend of the Late Elia," to the *Last Essays of Elia.*

Ostensibly a review of the life and works of the late Elia, the "Preface" provides Lamb an opportunity to consolidate and to outline more sharply the character of Elia and to defend indirectly the method of his art. Though the essays written before the "Preface" had given us a great deal of information about Elia, it was information that had been given us by Elia. To have the considered opinion of a friend would confirm our knowledge of Elia, since we would presume that a person writing about a late friend would tell us the truth. Pertinent to our more immediate discussion is Lamb's defense of Elia against the charge of egotism. Note first of all that these remarks follow an open criticism of Elia, thereby assuring the reader of the friend's honest and objective judgment:

> Egotistical they [the essays] have been pronounced by some who did not know, that what he tells us, as of himself, was often true only (historically) of another . . . If it be egotism to imply and twine with his own identity the griefs and affections of another—making himself many, or reducing many unto himself—then is

---

[23] Quoted by E. V. Lucas in his notes to *Works*, I, 433.

the skilful novelist, who all along brings in his hero, or heroine, speaking of themselves, the greatest egotist of all; who yet has never, therefore, been accused of that narrowness.

(II, 151)

Lamb could please his dramatic sense by writing under another name than his own, and, as Elia, he could write with more imaginative detachment about his own experiences, real or imagined.

Lamb probably enjoyed the prospect of creating and manipulating a character to whom he could return frequently. His persistent interest in Shakespeare and his later contemporaries reflected his abiding enjoyment of the dramatic. DeQuincey sees Lamb's instinct for the dramatic as the distinctive trait of his genius. "Lamb," he writes, "had the dramatic intellect and taste, perhaps, in perfection; of the epic he had none at all."[24] When a young man, Lamb had tried to write several plays, all of which were dismal failures. He even joined the audience in hissing the first and last performance of his farce "Mr. H—." Recognizing his inability to create and sustain a dramatic situation for the stage, Lamb probably saw the possibilities of adapting the character to his talents. The character of Elia gave him freedom in the use of autobiographical materials by dramatizing and distancing them. Through Elia he could be an objectifying dramatist rather than a self-conscious actor. Lamb realized the advantage of Elia as a defense against what he called the "indiviousness of a perpetual self-reference."[25]

Point of view constantly engaged the attention of the writers of the romantic period. On our perception of the use

---

[24] *The Works of Thomas De Quincey,* ed. David Masson (London: A. & C. Black, 1889-90), V, 236.

[25] Barnett, p. 44.

of point of view by Shelley, Blake, or Wordsworth depends
our understanding of their artistic intentions and their meta-
physical concerns. As strange as it may seem at first, the
qualities of character that Lamb attributes to Elia are relevant to his own conception of the imagination and to his
presentation of a particular point of view in the essays. Hu-
mility before the mysteries of existence, besides characteriz-
ing Elia's attitude toward life, is a quality in the imagination
of Lamb.

Elia maintains, so he claims, an open mind, with a ca-
pacity for change and an aversion for comfortable but in
reality unsatisfying resolutions and philosophies. His attitude
is not merely a desire to escape from the pressing demands
of daily existence, or an unwillingness to make decisions.
Elia rarely forces himself or an opinion; he usually offers his
judgments hesitantly and frequently qualifies them. A spirit
of self-denial and a sense of timidity, elements in the character of Elia, are designed to encourage the reader to enter
imaginatively into the essays. Lamb writes to Wordsworth:
"An intelligent reader finds a sort of insult in being told, I
will teach you how to think upon this subject. This fault, if I
am right, is in a ten-thousandth worse degree to be found in
Sterne and many, many novelists & modern poets, who con-
tinually put up a sign post to shew where you are to feel."[26]
Lamb does not want to persuade; he invites the reader into
his world to share with him in meditation some facets of existence, as shaped by the imagination.

Lamb provides an insight into the method of his art in
Elia's description of the anti-Caledonian habit of mind:

---

[26] *Letters,* I, 239.

There is an order of imperfect intellects (under which mine must
be content to rank) which in its constitution is essentially anti-
Caledonian. The owners of the sort of faculties I allude to, have
minds rather suggestive than comprehensive. They have no pre-
tences to much clearness or precision in their ideas, or in their
manner of expressing them. Their intellectual wardrobe (to confess fairly) has few whole pieces in it. They are content with frag-
ments and scattered pieces of Truth. She presents no full front to
them—a feature or side-face at the most. Hints and glimpses,
germs and crude essays at a system, is the utmost they pretend to.
(II, 59)

Elia's remarks are so casually and honestly delivered
that their significance is most probably overlooked. The essential Elian attitude is revealed here. He depreciates his
talents somewhat reluctantly, so he would have us believe,
placing himself in a rank of imperfect intellects. Yet when
Elia's remarks are placed in the context of Keats's discussion
of "negative capability," their significance as an expression of
an idea central to the romantic canon becomes startlingly
relevant. Keats describes "negative capability" in a letter to
his brothers:

That is when man is capable of being in uncertainties, mysteries,
doubts, without any irritable reaching after fact and reason—
Coleridge, for instance, would let go by a fine isolated verisimili-
tude caught from the Penetralium of mystery, from being incapable of remaining content with half knowledge.[27]

What is apparently a frank description by Elia of a
weaker sort of mind is, in fact, an expression of ideas similar
to those expressed by Keats. Lamb does not assault life or
shape it to preconceived notions. Mystery, the romantic
imagination realizes, will not be hunted down; it is not a nut

---

[27] Rollins, I, 193-194.

to be cracked by persistence; rather it will flash its truths into the mind.

Elia's essays are not crude attempts to shape imperfectly formed ideas; rather they are highly sophisticated works of art. And yet Lamb is interested in having his readers approach the essays with the same openness of mind that Elia describes as anti-Caledonian. They are in fact encouraged to do so by Elia's example. His practice suggests to the reader that he be satisfied with glimpses of truth and that he lay his judgment to rest so that his imagination can rightfully assert itself. If Elia's voice is low-keyed, it is in the hope that we will make the adjustment and read carefully.

The selection of apparently trivial objects and unpromising subjects as matter for the essays also serves Lamb's purposes. They are in keeping with the character of Elia. If Elia were to write of more ambitious matters, the illusion of his character would be destroyed. He is not much given to abstraction, nor to serious speculation, and fittingly the matter for his essays is drawn from observation of objects close around him, from personal memories, or from experiences with friends.

What Lamb excluded from his essays has received almost as much attention as what he included. Ian Jack writes that "in his essays, as in his letters, Lamb deliberately avoids whatever is urgent and disturbing; religion, sex, politics, suffering."[28] Lamb infrequently made of present matter a song. Mario Praz observes that Lamb did not include references to the major events of his time. He notes, for example, that in all of the essays there is not one reference to the Napoleonic

---

[28] *English Literature 1815-1832* (Oxford: Clarendon Press, 1963), p. 289.

Wars, the major event in Lamb's lifetime. Yet little effort has
been made to consider the significance of Lamb's choice of
some objects to the exclusion of others. What has often been
considered an unconscious effort to escape reality in his
failure to make reference to contemporary events in his essays is really a deliberate decision by Lamb and is in keeping
with the essay tradition.

The essay had traditionally excluded contemporary affairs or controversial subjects. Montaigne, for the most part,
avoided such matter. Disputable subjects are noticeably absent from the pages of the *Spectator* and the *Tatler*. How
often, for example, do the Marlborough Wars, or the victories
and defeats of the British armies, form topics for discussion?
When partisan issues were the subject of an essay, Addison
ridiculed them and thus hoped to discourage factionalism.
As the name *Spectator* implies, he was the withdrawn ob-
server who overheard and reported without becoming a
vociferous disputant. And so Lamb's avoidance of divisive
issues was traditional. Furthermore, though De Quincey was
experimenting with prose forms that would carry the more
soaring aspirations of the lyrical impulse, impassioned truths
and ambitious themes were still generally considered the
province of verse.

If Lamb left out of the essays certain immediate experiences or references to contemporary events, it was because
they were still too pressing to be considered imaginatively
or objectively. The reign of George the Fourth was one that
called for participation. Dissociation was difficult in that
period of turmoil, characterized by struggles and factions.
The *London Magazine* complained bitterly:

> The country is in a state of difficulty which leaves both the minis-
> terial party and the opposition, equally at a loss to suggest any

thing like probable means of relief; it is in a state of discontent
which has called, say ministers, for new and severe laws, and an
addition to the standing army. The industry of the nation is
divided against itself,—agriculture against manufacturers,—and
both are calling upon Parliament for protection. Our commerce is
assailed by unparalleled difficulties and competition, and prays
that a new legal system, likely to enable to cope with these, may
be adopted in regard to it. Our currency is in the very crisis of a
revolution . . . The public feeling has at length raised itself in
resistance to the sanguinary and unenlightened provisions which
disgrace our criminal code; and the legal position in which the
poor of the country are placed relatively to the other classes, is at
once disgraceful and destructive . . .

Such are a few of the more prominent points, claiming immediate consideration, and energetic measures on the part of
Parliament.[29]

Journalism and politics have always been closely allied, "but
at no time, perhaps, have the two been more closely in league
with the reviews and the magazines than between the peril-
ous days of 1789 and the Manchester Massacre of 1819—and
beyond."[30] Literary violence and personal vilification were
not uncommon. Frequently, a typical reviewer lost sight of
his critical bearings and judged a literary work more on his
like or dislike of the author's political, moral, or social opinions than on its literary merit. Lamb saw Byron scorned for
his atheism, the Cockney school ridiculed, and Wordsworth
and Coleridge attacked for their political apostasy. John Scott
died at the hands of John Gibson Lockhart's seconds during

---

[29] Josephine Bauer, *The London Magazine 1820-29* (Copenhagen:
Rosenkilde and Bagger, 1953), p. 19.

[30] William S. Ward, "Periodical Literature," in *Some British Romantics*, ed. James V. Logan, John E. Jordan, and Northrup Frye
(Columbus: Ohio State Univ. Press, 1966), p. 309.

a duel growing out of intemperate and untrue charges made by Scott against Lockhart.[31]

Sunday after Sunday, John and Leigh Hunt wrote criticisms of abuses of power in the cabinet and the crown, and were finally imprisoned for their persistence. Lamb himself participated in the affairs of the day. In 1812, he joined the Hunts in a caustic criticism of George the Fourth, then the Prince of Wales. The result of his contempt for the Regent was "The Triumph of the Whale," whose companions were all manner of monsters, sharks, and ink-fish. In the spring and summer of 1820, the same year that later saw the initiation of the Elia essays, Lamb again added to the attack on the Regent. Here is his sonnet, addressed to Mathew Wood, containing his sarcastic criticism of George Canning, a member of the King's ministry:

> Hold on thy course uncheck'd, heroic Wood!
>     Regardless what the player's son may prate,
>     Saint Stephens' fool, the Zany of Debate—
> Who nothing generous ever understood.
> London's twice Praetor! scorn the fool-born jest—
>     The stage's scum, and refuse of the players—
>     Stale topics against Magistrates and Mayors—
> City and Country both thy worth attest.
> Bid him leave off his shallow Eton wit,
>     More fit to sooth the superficial ear
>     Of drunken PITT, and that pickpocket Peer,
> When at their sottish orgies they did sit,
> Hatching mad counsels from inflated vein,
> Till England, and the nations, reeled with pain.
>                               (V, 105-106)

---

[31] Scott, the first editor of the *London Magazine,* unjustly charged Lockhart with the authorship of some caustic remarks, in *Blackwood's Magazine,* about Cockneys in literature. Scott maintained the truth of his charges in spite of Lockhart's persistent denials.

The public, one can assume, would be just as enmeshed in the events of the moment, which demand the engagement of strong passions and an evaluative response. Lamb considered it just as important to avoid disturbing subjects in consideration of the response that he wanted for the essays. The circumstances of the time and the heady atmosphere of the magazines most likely influenced Lamb, then, when he selected matter for his essays.

Great subjects that would engage the minds of statesmen, preachers, or lecturers are excluded, as are the recondite problems of the philosophers. While the romantic poets frequently went to nature or to the mysterious and the strange for their subjects and objects, Lamb consistently chose from the humble and the familiar. The essay materials are similar to the stuff of good talk: exchanges of tastes, reminiscences of youth, memories of dear friends, and discussions of books and art. Lamb appears to limit his analysis of feelings to minor emotions of regret, longings for the past, and desires for an escape from the tedious realities of daily life. Objects such as a piece of old china, playing cards, a sundial, or a water fountain add to the impression of unimportance, even triviality. There is an interesting account, in a review of contemporary periodical literature, of one reader's frustration at having the promise of the essays frequently dwindle to trivia:

> Elia in his happiest moods delights me; he is a fine soul; but when he is dull, his dullness sets human stupidity at defiance. He is like a well-bred, ill-trained pointer. He has a fine nose, but he won't or can't range. He keeps always close to your foot, and then he points larks and tit-mice. You see him snuffing and snoking and brandishing his tail with the most impassioned enthusiasm, and then drawn round into a semicircle he stands beautifully—dead set. You expect a burst of partridges, or a towering cock-pheasant,

when lo, and behold, away flits a lark, or you discover a mouse's nest, or there is absolutely nothing at all. Perhaps a shrew has been there the day before.[32]

Lamb would not have been at all surprised by the dismay of this reader, since he had purposefully designed the essays to twit readers searching for the great, the good, the beautiful, and the sublime.

Lamb also suspected that many would want to go to the essays for information. As we have seen, Elia takes pains to convince us of his ignorance, and so the reader who would look for practical considerations would also be disappointed, since practical matters are excluded. Lamb's essays are unlike the urbane essays by Steele and Addison, who deliberately set out to reform the manners and morals of the age and set themselves up as the disseminators and popularizers of vast amounts of knowledge. J. Lewis May, whose observations about the essays are often just but whose evaluation of them is frequently false, notes that "no writing was ever less purely intellectual, or less directly informative than the *Essays of Elia*. No one ever cared less than Lamb about writing to a theme, or keeping to his subject. Everything he says is true, but his truth is not the sort of truth that goes to the making of encyclopaedias."[33] Lamb develops the essay as an expressive and aesthetic, not an informative medium, and he underlines his purposes by his choice of materials. The unobtrusive materials are designed to serve Lamb's purpose not to have "a palpable design upon us,"[34] to use Keats's phrase.

Like the other romantics, Lamb was concerned with expanding the list of materials that could be considered as sub-

---

[32] *Life*, II, 537.
[33] *Charles Lamb: A Study* (London: Geoffrey Bles, 1934), p. 193.
[34] Rollins, I, 224.

ject matter for art and for the aesthetic experience. A cup of
china, or roast pig, Lamb suggested, can be considered as fit
subjects for the imagination. Prose, the familiar essayists felt,
should be extending its imaginative range, as poetry had been
doing. Lamb was widening the field of objects that could be
considered aesthetic.

Lamb's aims in the essays are similar to those of De
Quincey in his series of essays titled "On Murder Considered
as One of the Fine Arts." The preposterous nature of the
proposal provides a clue to De Quincey's purposes. He writes
of his subject: "Murder, for instance, may be laid hold of by
its moral handle (as it generally is in the pulpit and at the
Old Bailey), and *that*, I confess, is its weak side; or it may
also be treated *aesthetically*, as the Germans call it—that is,
in relation to good taste."[35] He chooses murder as his subject
to dramatize the difference between a moral treatment and
an aesthetic treatment of an action. Although De Quincey
pretends to lecture on the aesthetics of murder, he is lec-
turing on aesthetics, distinguishing between imaginatively
meditating on an experience and reacting to it in real life.
Lamb chose to write about common experiences and simple
emotions, and he wanted the reader to experience them
aesthetically, that is, not to enter into them as if they were a
re-enactment of reality. And he could partially assure himself of this response by choosing materials that would be least
likely to engage the reader's moral and critical faculties.

The style of the essays appears artificial and mannered.[36]

---

[35] Masson, XIII, 13.

[36] My discussion of style is limited to the argument of this chapter,
and so it is by no means complete. The style in the essays is an extremely supple medium in Lamb's hands. It is an appropriate vehicle
of the ideas and feelings that inform the essays. When the easy, urbane

Obsolete terms, uncommon inversions, eccentricities, and the use of "thee" and "thy" appear in enough essays to give readers a sense of the oddity of the style. Elia's friend confirms our judgment in the "Preface," where he says of the essays: "Crude they are, I grant you—a sort of unlicked, incondite things—villainously pranked in an affected array of antique modes and phrases" (II, 151). De Quincey notices the absence of "rhythmus, or pomp of cadence, or sonorous ascent of clauses, in the structure" of the sentences in the essays, and he adds that such effects of art were "as much thrown away upon *him* [Lamb] as the voice of the charmer upon the deaf adder."[37]

De Quincey is both right and wrong. Sonorous sentences are generally absent from Lamb's essays, but not because Lamb was incapable of them or because he had a tin ear. Lamb could, when his art called for it, write a sentence as rhythmic as any of the sentences of his contemporaries. Consider, for example, the closing sentence of "Mackery End, in Hertfordshire." Elia has been describing a visit to his cousin in Hertfordshire, who then takes him, Bridget, and a friend to meet her mother and sister Gladmans:

> With what corresponding kindness we were received by them also—how Bridget's memory exalted by the occasion, warmed into a thousand half-obliterated recollections of things and persons, to my utter astonishment, and her own—and to the astoundment of

---

manner of the earlier essayists is wanted, Lamb can recreate it effectively, as in "The Genteel Style in Writing," where Lamb imitates the style under discussion. Or he can adapt it to the *jeux d'esprit* of "To the Shade of Elliston," or to the sober reality of dreams and wishes in "Dream Children; A Reverie." A spirit of exaggeration and lofty words add a sense of grandeur to the recollections of youth in "The South-Sea House."

[37] Masson, V, 235.

B. F. who sat by, almost the only thing that was not a cousin
there,—old effaced images of more than half-forgotten names and
circumstances still crowding back upon her, as words written in
lemon come out upon exposure to a friendly warmth,—when I
forget all this, then may my country cousins forget me; and Bridget no more remember, that in the days of weakling infancy I was
her tender charge—as I have been her care in foolish manhood
since—in those pretty pastoral walks, long ago, about Mackery
End, in Hertfordshire.

(II, 78-79)

The pace of the sentence is carefully modulated to accompany the movement of a mind kindling to warm recollections, mounting to a climax, pivoting at "when I forget," and
calmly subsiding into a mood of tender regret.

George L. Barnett's examination of Lamb's frequent
revisions of the essays also reveals how sensitive Lamb was
to sound, since a good number of the corrections were made
for euphony. If there are not the involute rhythms of De
Quincey's prose in the *Essays of Elia,* it is not that Lamb
was incapable of them, but rather that he fashioned a prose
answering to his artistic needs.

Lamb deliberately wanted to create the illusion of ec-
centricity of style. As with the other facets of his art, the
reasons are several and related. Immediately following his
description—already quoted—of the style of the essays as affected, the writer of the "Preface" adds that the essays had
not been Elia's, "if they had been other than such; and better
it is, that a writer should be natural in a self-pleasing quaintness, than to affect a naturalness (so called) that should be
strange to him" (II, 151). The style is adapted to the character of Elia; there is no sense of discrepancy between his character and the style of the essays by his hand. In short, Lamb
creates a distinctive Elian voice and a style reflecting a personal vision. There is also an oblique reference in the passage

to the romantic doctrine of sincerity. The romantic canon demanded that a writer develop a personal and unique voice; to have done otherwise would have been false. However, Lamb suggests, it would be more affected to feign a naturalness than to write in a style that, though apparently artificial, is in fact expressive of the author. Lamb, too, probably indirectly measured Wordsworth's definition of the language of the new literature, that it be "the very language of men."[38]

The strangeness of style also has a rhetorical effect similar to the outcome of Elia's many professions of ignorance. Artificiality of style adds to the illusion that the essays are oddities and creations of no practical use. The essays are, the style suggests, artifacts. And the spirit of exaggeration and self-importance frequently found reflected in De Quincey's style is generally avoided by Lamb to dissociate himself from any tone of gravity and solemnity.[39]

Lamb found the essay form particularly suited to his various needs and aims as an artist. A strong factor directing Lamb to use the form was his personality, since the essay is highly fitted to spontaneity and subjectivity. I noted earlier that Lamb pointed out his inclination to full self-expression in a letter to Coleridge. The essay was a plastic form. Men as various in temperaments and talents as Bacon, Montaigne, Cowley, Addison, and Swift had used the form. Its suppleness was, undoubtedly, one of the reasons why Lamb chose it for the most important work of his career, since he could

---

[38] *The Prose Works of William Wordsworth,* ed. Alexander B. Grosart (London: Edward Moxon, 1876), II, 84.

[39] Or if pompous expressions are present, as in "The South-Sea House," they are skillfully related to the form, the matter, and themes of the essay.

adapt it to anecdote, development of the character, reminiscence, to the froth of his mind as well as its more sober imaginings. One has only to read in turn the essays "The Old Benchers of the Inner Temple," "Dream Children; A Reverie," "The Genteel Style in Writing," "To the Shade of Elliston," and "The Praise of Chimney-Sweepers" to appreciate Lamb's diverse handling of the essay form.

His work at the India House left him little time for any concerted effort. "He had not," writes Edmund Blunden, "the conditions of life in which he might envisage a great construction of the imaginative faculty, therefore he kept away from any harassed and uncertain attempts."[40] And too, the difficulties of composition probably influenced Lamb to choose a limited form. He found it difficult to write regularly, and he wrote slowly, often with difficulty. Many of his apparently spontaneous investions were the result of long labors. Mary Lamb, in a letter to Sarah Stoddart, writes of the progress of the *Tales from Shakespeare* and describes her brother's hand in the project:

> Charles has written Macbeth, Othello, King Lear, and has begun Hamlet; you would like to see us, as we often sit, writing on one table (but not on one cushion sitting), like Hermia and Helena in the Midsummer's Night's Dream; or, rather, like an old literary Darby and Joan: I taking snuff, and he groaning all the while, and saying he can make nothing of it, which he always says till he has finished, and then he finds out he has made something of it.[41]

Yet to suggest that Lamb could have produced only what he did write is foolish, since it makes Lamb's art mainly a result of circumstances and necessity. Lamb did not write

[40] Edmund Blunden, *Charles Lamb and His Contemporaries* (Hamden: Archon Books, 1967), p. 150.
[41] *Letters*, II, 10.

any single work of length because of lack of invention or power of mind; rather, "it was his essential decision or criticism that restrained him."[42] The more important reasons for Lamb's choice must be found in his desire to create a context for the essays and in his efforts to expand the limits of what could be considered an appropriate form for a man's artistic imaginings.

The personal, subjective manner is a distinctive feature of the familiar essay, as developed by Lamb and others, but what most characterizes the familiar essay, I believe, was its growing importance as a literary form, the history of which can be traced into the late nineteenth century.[43] Readers of magazines during Lamb's time would still be familiar with the conventions and traditions of the Addisonian essay. Although a medium for entertainment in the eighteenth century, the essay's most characteristic office lay in its modest didacticism and light satire of the weakness of contemporary vices and weaknesses. Even Goldsmith's essays incline toward moralizing. The eighteenth-century essayists worked hard to create an atmosphere of reality in their works. They described figures familiar to the London world—the beau, the woman of fashion—and recorded the life, opinions, and fashionable ideas of the time. And they published letters from supposed correspondents and reported conversations of clubs and coffeehouses.

Marie Hamilton Law has demonstrated that the familiar essays of Hunt, De Quincey, Hazlitt, and Lamb retained most of the elements that characterize their predecessors'

---

[42] Edmund Blunden, *Charles Lamb and His Contemporaries,* p. 150.

[43] See *The Art of Victorian Prose,* ed. George Levine and William Madden (London: Oxford Univ. Press, 1968).

essays.[44] The informal, conversational tone, the treatment of trivial matter in a humorous way, and the use of the character and anecdote are found in both the periodical essays and the familiar essay. But the prose writers of the romantic period saw and enlarged the possibilities of the essay as an aesthetic form, worthy of their best efforts as artists. It would be strange, indeed, that a period which witnessed the creation and the development of new verse forms should not also see a similar experimentation in prose. De Quincey was experimenting with the confession, the autobiography, the lyrical romance, prose poems, and the essay to give expression to his personal vision. Most of these forms generally reflect the greater depth and breadth of De Quincey's genius, his ability to sustain the imaginative activity for greater periods of time. Lamb's was a more limited art, though not less artful.

The perfection of the familiar essay was not the result of isolated labors, but the creation of minds nourished and sustained by the new periodicals of the early nineteenth century. The years between 1802 and 1820 were a transitional period in the history of the periodical magazine, since during that period editors and writers worked to make the magazine a medium of high literary standard. Men such as Leigh Hunt of the *Reflector* and the *Examiner*, and John Scott of the *London Magazine* stressed literature, drama, criticism, and the fine arts more than the older periodical magazines did. The contributors to the *London* met at intervals to exchange friendship and ideas. Besides Lamb, this group at the *London* dinners included B. W. Procter, Allan Cunningham, Hood, George Darley, John Clare, Hartley Coleridge, Hazlitt, De Quincey, J. H. Reynolds, and others.

---

[44] *The English Familiar Essay in the Early Nineteenth Century* (New York: Russell & Russell, 1965), pp. 57-103.

These men witnessed and were instrumental in creating a new type of magazine, more literary than the *Monthly Magazine,* the *Literary Magazine,* or *Blackwood's Magazine,* which generally were digesters and transmitters of information. The new magazine gradually eliminated chronicle matter and turned its efforts to entertainment. There was an increasing interest in the essay as an art, not merely a journalistic form. Leigh Hunt sounds the hopes and ambitions of the new magazines in his description of the aims of the *London Journal:*

> We wished to create one corner and field of periodical literature, in which men might be sure of hope and cheerfulness, and of the cultivation of peaceful and flowery thoughts, without the accompaniment of anything inconsistent with them; we knew that there was a desire at the bottom of every human heart to retain a faith in such thoughts, and to see others believe in the religion and recommend it; and heartily have anxious as well as happy readers in this green and beautiful England responded to our belief . . . The *London Journal* is a sort of park for rich and poor, for the reflecting and well-intentioned of all sorts; where every one can be alone, or in company, as he thinks fit, and see, with his mind's eye, a succession of Elysian sights, ancient and modern, and as many familiar objects to boot, or hear nothing but birds and waterfalls, or the comforted beatings of his own heart,—all effected for him by no greater magician than Good Faith and a little reading.[45]

Hunt's wishes came to fruition in Lamb's essays. Lamb is not, then, an oddity out of the mainstream of English literature.

Elia, however, did not have a very high opinion of his works. Frequently associated with the portrait of gentle Elia is the belief that the essays are minor achievements, at best the delicate products of a precious craftsman. This opinion

---

[45] *Ibid.,* p. 54.

is partly the result of Lamb's method of presentation and is apparently justified by Elia's diffidence toward the essays and by his profession of their triviality.

The form is fitted to the character of Elia; it is an unpretentious form for an unassuming clerk. He refers to his essays as his recreations and points to the folios that he filled up in the service of the South Sea House as his works. "In thee remain," he says to his folios, "and not in the obscure collection of some wandering bookseller, my 'works'!" (II, 197). Of his first essay, "The South-Sea House," he says to his readers: "I tried to divert thee with some half-forgotten humours of some old clerks defunct, in an old house of business" (II, 7). Neither the subject of the essay nor his judgment of his intentions are ambitious. Elia underplays his achievement. The judgment of that dependable friend of Elia, the writer of the "Preface" to the *Last Essays of Elia,* echoes Elia's attitude. He writes as if his remarks were representative of the public opinion of the essays: "I am now at liberty to confess, that much which I have heard objected to my late friend's writings was well-founded. Crude they are, I grant you—a sort of unlicked, incondite things—villainously pranked in an affected array of antique modes and phrases" (II, 151). Can we doubt the judgment of a man who is so obviously honest? Readers and critics have generally accepted Elia's judgment at face value and made it the basis for their own judgments of the essays.

Lamb's remarks about the essays, however, in letters and in conversations, the judgment of his contemporaries, and the success of the essays, contradict Elia's statements about his achievement. Lamb said in response to Eliza Cook's declared admiration of the essays: "You are very polite and kind. The public has been very indulgent towards them. Whatever their faults, I endeavored to write them with discrimination and care. The little *Essays,* by Elia, have not been despised."[46] In fact, their popularity was so great that Lamb, according to Barry Cornwall, was paid two or three times the amount of the other contributors to the *London.*

That Lamb's practice is contrary to what the friend says about the essays is also evident from the numerous revisions made by Lamb in the essays. There are many letters to the editors of the *London* and the *New Monthly* magazines requesting last-minute changes in his contributions. George L. Barnett examined a number of the extant manuscripts of the essays and found that Lamb revised his work constantly. He strove to improve his writings, no matter how many times he transcribed from an earlier version. He describes his careful writing habits to Robert Southey: "I am as slow as a Fleming painter when I compose anything."[47] Lamb exerted himself even over what he would have considered minor achievements. Barnett points to revisions made in a minor prose piece titled "Dog Days" to illustrate the painstaking efforts Lamb took with all his compositions.

What, then, are we to make of the contradictions between Elia's remarks, the judgment of the author of the "Preface," and Lamb's remarks and practice? Elia's opinion of his works and his friend's confirmation of it are another part of Lamb's rhetorical method to create a context that will shape the reader's response. If the essays are presented as the modest, even trivial, scribblings of an obscure South Sea clerk, the reader will most likely assume that they should not be taken too seriously. The unassuming form itself suggests

---

[46] Blunden, p. 192.
[47] *Letters,* I, 132.

the same reaction. This deception of his readers is part of Lamb's endeavor to blunt the voracious appetites of men and women looking for information, a reflection of real life, moral truths, or knowledge about the practical affairs of men in the essays. We have been forewarned. If we bring to the essays the same preconceptions with which we approach the periodical essayists or the articles in the more conservative magazines of the time, we will be greatly disappointed. By pretending to attempt little, Lamb was free to try a great many new things.

Finally, the limited form of the essay is superbly fitted to a mind that called itself anti-Caledonian. More ambitious forms would suggest a framework of thought sustaining a fully developed theme or matter. The essay is admirably suited to the quick glance, the intuition, the momentary enjoyment.

Lamb used the character of Elia, an amiable eccentric who claims to know very little, the unpretentious form of the essay, eccentricities of style, and a selection of humble objects and unpromising subjects to create the illusion that the essays are outside the fluctuations of reality. These rhetorical devices also served him as solutions to the difficulties posed for the romantic artist who turned to the subjective voice for the materials of his art.

The essays of Elia are Lamb's spots of time, and the total body of his essays is his major romantic work. In them Lamb and his reader can meet again and again; he is invited to return to them "for the thousandth time" (II, 75). They provide momentary refuges from the world of choice and will. The character of Elia and the essay form provide links, unifying all the essays, and both create a personal voice for Lamb that mediates between him and his public.

With Elia as our guide, it is time to approach the essays in a spirit of idle contemplation.

# II

## THE GROWTH OF THE IMAGINATION

*"Blakesmoor in H---shire"*
*"The Old Benchers of the Inner Temple"*

M AN, architecture, and artifacts, not nature, provide Charles Lamb with the most frequent themes, objects, and symbols in the *Essays of Elia*. The landscape of Elia's memory is filled with evidence of the presence of man in his universe. When nature does provide a setting, it is domesticated. And the gardens are filled with artifacts, such as fountains, sundials, and statues. Wordsworth returns again and again to the mountains, rivers, and valleys of his childhood for the materials of his poetry; Lamb most often uses urban settings and man-made objects for the materials and symbols of his essays. Buildings are frequently used as settings in the essays.

The South-Sea House, the Inner Temple, Blakesmoor, and Mackery End each has an essay named after it. These essays generally exhibit a similar method of organization. They begin in the present, enter into a remembrance of the past, characterized by a sense of holiness and tranquillity, and return to the present. This circular movement corresponds to the activity of the imagination: it frees itself from present concerns, turns within a spirit of contemplation, and then returns to present reality. This method is not explicitly defined or rigorously followed, but its outline is sufficiently present in each essay to warrant observation and comment.

The situation and setting of the essays provide the materials for the meditation, give shape to the activity of the imagination, and frequently serve as symbols for the results of the mind's activity. The narrative and setting incarnate the process of thought; the visible and the mental, the objective and the subjective fuse. A discussion of "Blakesmoor in H---shire" and "The Old Benchers of the Inner Temple" will demonstrate Lamb's method and concerns in these essays where buildings provide the setting. In both essays Lamb returns to his childhood settings for his subject matter and traces the growth of his imagination. Like Wordsworth, he associates vivid memories with specific places, and his recollections are the source of inspiration and grace.

A fine old family mansion is the setting of "Blakesmoor in H---shire." Elia opens the essay with several general remarks:

> I do not know a pleasure more affecting than to range at will over the deserted apartments at some fine old family mansion. The traces of extinct grandeur admit of a better passion than envy: and contemplations on the great and good, whom we fancy in

succession to have been its inhabitants, weave for us illusions, in-
compatible with the bustle of modern occupancy, and vanities of
foolish present aristocracy.[1]

Elia enforces the contrast by comparing the difference
of feeling that attends us between visiting a deserted and a
crowded church. In the latter some chance distraction "puts
us by our best thoughts, disharmonizing the place and the
occasion" (II, 154). But in an empty church a man free from
"disturbing emotions" and "cross conflicting comparisons"
drinks "in the tranquillity of the place," till he becomes as
"fixed and motionless as the marble effigies that kneel and
weep around" (II, 154) him. A spirit of silence, solitude,
and tranquillity is necessary for imaginative contemplation.

There are Wordsworthian and Keatsian echoes in Elia's
descriptions of the pleasures of solitude. The country church,
filled with pregnant silence, provides the occasion for the
mind to feed on the tranquil beauty of holiness and solitude,
until the imagination experiences a sense of stasis, a state of
being that is generally associated by the romantics with immortality. Elia describes a cessation of activity and a partak-
ing in permanence. He would become as motionless as the
marble effigies and share in their permanence; the statues
would share in his emotions and weep around him. The imagination contemplates at the same time contradictory desires
for permanence and vitality. Yet the experience of the understanding, which comprehends that vitality leads finally to
death, and the activity of the imagination, which creates

---

[1] *The Works of Charles and Mary Lamb*, ed. E. V. Lucas (London: Methuen, 1903-5), II, 153. Volume number and page numbers
for subsequent quotations from the *Works* will be given in the text.

symbols of immortality, are not at odds. Through the imagination the artist creates a symbol of dynamic stasis, a state
of being that fuses permanence and vitality.

After his general observations on the pleasures of solitude Elia turns to particular memories of this pleasure associated with Blakesmoor. He relates a recent visit to the remains of the old house that had impressed him deeply as a
child. He went to Blakesmoor probably expecting to renew
the pleasure of his childhood, but he found upon his arrival
that the old mansion had been pulled down recently. Elia is
confronted with an interesting situation: will be be able to
relive his experiences, although the mansion has been demol-
ished?

A vague notion persists in Elia that the mansion could
not have been completely destroyed. The reasons for his
feelings will become distinct as the essay proceeds. What
remains for Elia is some germ to be revivified, that is, his
memories of his visits to Blakesmoor in infancy. Whereas in
the description of his contemplations in an empty church and
a deserted mansion, Elia's imagination feeds on actual settings for its materials, his recollections of Blakesmoor energize his imagination and enable him to reconstitute the old
mansion. Memory, as in Wordsworth's work, holds out the
promise of continuity and a way of overcoming the effects of
time. Elia's memories of the mansion are stronger than the
fact of its destruction. The revival of particular memories
parallels the reconstruction of the house in his imagination.

Elia feels "that so much solidity with magnificence could
not have been crushed all at once into the mere dust and
rubbish" (II, 154) that he finds. The few bricks that remain
provide little clue to the layout of the house, its gates, and its
surroundings. While he dwells on the meager remains of

what was once so stately, Elia associates the death of man
with the destruction of the house. "Death does not shrink up
his human victim at this rate. The burnt ashes of a man weigh
more in their proportion" (II, 154), he writes. He seems to
ask: how can the human spirit rise again, if something as
magnificent and solid as the old house is irrevocably destroyed? The physical remains—a few bricks and a man's
ashes—correspond to the seeds of memory. In memory and
the imagination Elia will find the means to confront the destruction of the house and man's death. Elia appears to re-
verse the general process that one would expect; he hopes to
suggest the resurrection of man by reconstructing the house.

Elia imagines what he would have done had he been
present at the destruction of the house: "Had I seen these
brick-and-mortar knaves at their process of destruction, at
the plucking of every panel I should have felt the varlets at
my heart" (II, 154). The dismantling of the house would
have been felt by him as the destruction of his own body.
The process of recollection, however, is a rebuilding. His
imagined protests and pleas to "spare a plank at least out of
the cheerful store-room" (II, 154) prod the memory to recall
specific parts of the mansion. He used to sit in the hot win-
dow seat of the store-room and read Cowley, "with the grass-
plat before, and the hum and flappings of that one solitary
wasp that ever haunted it about me—it is in mine ears now,
as oft as summer returns" (II, 154). As Elia vividly recalls
parts of the house and associates specific memories with each
room, he returns increasingly to the viewpoint of the child
Elia. Elia's focus of description has moved from the grounds
of the mansion to the interior of the house and parallels the
movement of the mind into the recesses of memory and imagination, wherein Elia will recreate the world of his youth.

He moves on confidently: "Why, every plank and pannel of that house for me had magic in it" (II, 154). He does not hesitate in his descriptions or grope for recollections; memory generates memory. Distinctness and exactness of detail, generally associated with Wordsworth's descriptions of scenes and recollections, also characterize Elia's remembrances. He describes in turn other rooms and their furnishings, no longer as if he is reconstituting what had vanished, but as if he were describing what still exists. When a child he used to peep half-fearfully from behind his covers at the tapestries in the bedrooms. Although representations of stories from mythology, they were as real to the child as any of his other surroundings. Describing scenes from Ovid, the tapestries played a part similar to the role played by Arabian tales in Wordsworth's childhood; they fostered the growth of his mind. There are only participles in Elia's description of the scenes on the tapestries: "Actaeon in mid sprout, with the unappeasable prudery of Diana; and the still more provoking, and almost culinary coolness of Dan Phoebus, eel-fashion, deliberately divesting of Marsyas" (II, 155). The actions are ever going on, as if they were not subject to the passing of time, because they enjoy the immortality of art. Elia's curious understatement of the brutal matter of both tapestries—"divesting" is a euphemism for flaying alive—suggests that art drains the actions of Actaeon and Dan Phoebus of their horror, so that they can be contemplated free from conflicting emotions.

The child Elia was fostered "by beauty and by fear"[2] alike. The recollections have a sort of progression, from the

---

[2] William Wordsworth, *The Prelude*, ed. Ernest de Selincourt (Oxford: Clarendon Press, 1926), p. 19.

"cheerful store-room," to the "stern bright visages" of the
tapestries, and to "that haunted room—in which old Mrs.
Battle died—whereinto I have crept, but always in the day-
time, with a passion of fear; and a sneaking curiosity, terror-
tainted, to hold communication with the past" (II, 155). As
Elia describes his experiences in the many rooms of the mansion—the house of memory too—we begin to realize that he
is describing the "fair seed-time"[3] of his soul. A lonely child,
he "had the range at will of every apartment, knew every
nook and corner, wondered and worshipped everywhere"
(II, 155). Roaming through the house and feeding on its
objects and the spirit of solitude, he learned the lessons of
"love, and silence, and admiration" (II, 155). He nourished
his emotions in the presence of the house.

The spirit of the place was so strong that the child never
ventured beyond the confines of the house. Since he was content with his situation, the extensive prospects near the house,
with which he was familiar by hearsay, did not appeal to
him. Indeed, far from desiring to roam, he would have drawn
the boundaries of his confines ever closer about him: "So far
from a wish to roam, I would have drawn, methought, still
closer the fences of my chosen prison; and have been
hemmed in by a yet securer cincture of those excluding garden walls" (II, 155). As Elia returns deeper into his childhood, the dimensions of the mansion shrink. From the solid
magnificence of the earlier descriptions of the mansion, Elia's
recollections have descended to snug firesides and frugal
boards. "I was here as in a lonely temple" (II, 155), he
writes. "Snug firesides—the low-built roof—parlours ten feet
by ten—frugal boards, and all the homeliness of home—these

---

[3] *Ibid.*

were the condition of my birth—the wholesome soil which I was planted in" (II, 155). The days of his infancy were characterized by a sense of security, happiness, simplicity, and frugality. And these qualities were the conditions of his spiritual birth. As does Wordsworth in *The Prelude,* Lamb is, in effect, retracing the history of the growth of his mind. At the same time, he is exercising that mind in reconstituting the mansion. Because he was planted in propitious soil, his imagination, drawing on his memories and on the virtues fostered in childhood, can create without the props of its earlier affections being actually present. He creates temples of the mind, and he has answered his question: *"How shall they build it up again?"* (II, 155). Elia has re-created the mansion; now he will inhabit it as its true inhabitant and real heir.

As he had revived the mansion in his memory and had appropriated it in his imagination, so too he revives the ancestry of the house by appropriating it to himself. A shift in tone accompanies Elia's comments on gentility. He is more forceful and argumentative, as if to demonstrate his pride in himself. An antiquary without any sort of pedigree may "warm himself into as gay a vanity as those who do inherit them. The claims of birth are ideal merely, and what herald shall go about to strip me of an idea? Is it trenchant to their swords? can it be hacked off as a spur can? or torn away like a tarnished garter?" (II, 156). The failing fortunes of a great family and the instability of the trappings and ornament of nobility are contrasted with the idea of gentility. Just as a sense of love and admiration was nourished in the house, so too the idea of gentility and pride of ancestry were inculcated there. Great families and their genealogies should arouse in each man pride in his ancestry, that is, in his common ancestry with the sons of Adam. These families appeal to us because they are particular examples of each man's splendid past. Contemplation of great genealogies and uninterrupted lineage should be a boost to each man's conception of himself. "What to us the uninterrupted current of their bloods," Elia writes, "if our own did not answer within us to a cognate and correspondent elevation" (II, 156).

It was because of thoughts such as these that Elia in childhood so often pored over the mystic characters of the tattered escutcheon that hung upon the walls of the stairs at Blakesmoor mansion. He writes that he gazed on its mystic characters, its "emblematic supporters, with their prophetic 'Resurgam'—till, every dreg of peasantry purging off, I received into myself Very Gentility" (II, 156). Those bound by the knowledge of their senses would have seen only decay. The boy, however, fed his mind on ideas of resurrection and continuity. Amidst the decay of the accidental accouterments associated with gentility, he learned the concept of permanence, represented by the idea of nobility. The shield's prophetic promise was immediate in its assurance to him. He passed it each evening on his way to bed. His awakening each new day fulfilled the shield's promise.

Elia's appropriation of the pedigree of Blakesmoor to himself had nothing to do with the fortunes of his birth. "To have the feelings of gentility, it is not necessary to have been born gentle" (II, 156), Elia remarks. The fading rags and colors of the trophy indicated that it was two centuries old. At that date Elia's ancestor might have been a shepherd, feeding his master's flocks. But that thought does not stop Elia from appropriating to himself the feelings of nobility. The mere transmission of blood from generation to generation is no assurance of real gentry; it depends rather on an imaginative grasp of the idea of nobility. Furthermore, the present owners of the mansion have little reason to complain of Elia's actions, since they had abandoned the place, leaving it tenantless. It is he who resides there, enjoys the mansion, and keeps alive the deeds of the ancestors. He is the heir, since he has resurrected the house in his mind and carries its memories, hallowed by time and the imagination, with him. And so he is "the true descendant of those old W---s; and not the present family of that name, who had fled the old waste places" (II, 156).

Having completed his identification with the ancestors of Blakesmoor, as earlier he had identified himself with its buildings, he now catalogues his possessions. The objects that Elia first singles out as his own are portraits, a noble Marble Hall, and the busts of the Twelve Caesars—all art objects. Death has ironically given those represented by the paintings and the Caesars a form of immortality. This paradox, first noticed in childhood, persists in Elia's mind, since the image of the marble busts suggests the earlier image of the effigies on the tombs. Elia is recounting the reception into his mind of the idea and images of immortality found in the products of the imagination. As he gives his own family name to the portraits, he imagines them reaching forward to acknowledge the new relationship and their hope for immortality, since posterity is one form of immortality. They gain life in the mind of Elia, who assures them a sort of immortality by including them in the essay. In a similar fashion the stately busts in marble enshrined the faces and the lives of the Caesars. They stood "in the coldness of death, yet freshness of immortality" (II, 157). Art has the permanence of death; life the impermanence of vitality. Lamb implies that Elia's immortality is assured him by the essays. If we appropriate Elia and his work to us, as he had identified himself with the house and its inhabitants, he and his essays will live in our imagination.

As previously Elia had approached the house from the outside, moving to the inside, so now he moves from the inside to the outside of the house, to its gardens and beyond. A sense of greatness, learned from contemplation of the idea of gentility, evidently widened his horizons, since he now includes the gardens beyond the strict confines of the house in mention of his experience. His vision and experience expand to include the fruit garden, an ampler garden behind that with its flowerpots showing the effects of time, to "verdant quarters backwarder still," and to the "firry wilderness" beyond that (II, 157). The experiences of gentility and continuity taught him to identify himself with objects greater than himself and suggested to him the hope of immortality, so that he can approach the world of experience and reality with confidence. At the center of the firry wilderness he worshipped an antique image, a "fragmental mystery" (II, 157); god or goddess he did not know. Even in the center of the wilderness he found evidence of man's hand.

Elia breaks off his recitation of memories and ends the essay with several questions and a hesitant expression of a hope:

Was it for this, that I kissed my childish hands too fervently in your idol worship, walks and windings of *Blakesmoor!* for this, or what sin of mine, has the plough passed over your pleasant places? I sometimes think that as men, when they die, do not die all, so of their extinguished habitations there may be a hope—a germ to be revivified.

(II, 157)

Elia's question obscures his achievement, since his hopes have already been fulfilled. But it is the reader, not Elia, who recognizes the dramatic movement of the essay. We are not given final thoughts or conclusions but rather the materials of Elia's meditation. Following the direction, the implications, and the suggestions of Elia's meditation we share with Lamb the creation of the essay. Elia first uses the name Blakesmoor midway through the essay, in the passage describing the escutcheon and its "Resurgam." His continued mention of the name in the last paragraph, wherein he asks why the mansion has passed away, suggests that he still feels the existence and reality of Blakesmoor—the Blakesmoor of memory and imagination. The essay fills the promise of what he considers to be a possibility. Elia's imagination, nurtured by his experiences at Blakesmoor, revivifies the germs of memory and assures the continuation of his memories by giving them the permanence of art.

The mansion achieves the immortality of art. Elia's art, like the busts of the Twelve Caesars, stands "in the coldness of death, yet freshness of immortality." The destruction of the buildings occasions their reconstitution in art; their destruction is their guarantee of immortality. It is Elia's implied hope that man's death also holds the promise of immortality.

Elia has shown the origins of his imagination and its independence of immediate experience. That he can revivify past experiences and have an imaginary experience similar to the real pleasure of walking through deserted mansions or empty churches reveals to him the liberating powers of the imagination. Not dependent on reality alone, the imagination shows to Elia the way to freedom from disturbing emotions and "cross conflicting comparisons." The mind can create its own temple and worship within. Yet we must remember that Elia does not retreat from reality; rather, he views reality imaginatively, drawing uncommon knowledge from common objects.

"The Old Benchers of the Inner Temple" is divided into two main parts and ends with an explanatory postscript. In the first half of the essay Elia relates his childhood memories of the Inner Temple and its surroundings; in the second half he describes his recollections of the Benchers of the Temple. Elia was born and lived the first seven years of his life there. Its buildings and gardens are of his "oldest recollections" (II, 82). His memories of the spot are so pleasant that he repeats no verses to himself more frequently than those of Spenser, where he speaks of the Temple:

Where now the studious lawyers have their bowers,
There whylome wont the Templer knights to bide,
Till they decayd through pride.[4]

These lines lend a sense of antiquity to Elia's observations and indirectly tell us that others before him had enjoyed the pleasures of the Temple. The quotation also partially bridges the movement of Elia's mind from the present to the past. Furthermore, the lines suggest that Elia is sharing in a community of hallowed memories associated with the Temple.

Because it is such an elegant spot in the city, Elia warms to the thought of some visitor coming to the Temple: "What a transition for a countryman visiting London for the first time—the passing from the crowded Strand or Fleet-street, by unexpected avenues, into its magnificent ample squares, its classic green recesses!" (II, 83). Although the reference to activity and noise is slight, it is no less significant, since the

[4] Quoted by Lamb in *Works*, II, 82.

imagined passing from the street to the recesses of the Temple signals the passing into the world of the imagination and memory. There is, to use Lascelles Abercrombie's definition of romanticism, a "withdrawal from outer experience in order to concentrate on inner experience."[5] The sense of wonder increases, as the Temple and its garden are seen more and more from the viewpoint of the young boy:

> What a cheerful, liberal look hath that portion of it, which, from three sides, overlooks the greater garden: that goodly pile
>
> Of building strong, albeit of Paper hight,
>
> confronting, with massy contrast, the lighter, older, more fantastically shrouded one, named of Harcourt, with the cheerful Crown-office Row (place of my kindly engendure), right opposite the stately stream, which washes the garden-foot with her yet scarcely trade-polluted waters, and seems but just weaned from her Twickenham Naiades! a man would give something to have been born in such places. What collegiate aspect has that fine Elizabethan hall, where the fountain plays, which I have made to rise and fall, how many times! to the astoundment of the young urchins, my contemporaries.

(II, 83)

The child's sense of awe and spirit of exaggeration are accompanied by a shift in phraseology and diction. An impression of quaintness and archaism is added to the spirit of the essay by the use of a phrase such as "named of Harcourt," and a word such as "engendure."

Like Spenser before him, Elia gives the features of the Temple grandeur and value. Although the setting is limited— the Temple and its gardens are walled in—there is no sense of confinement. The magnificence and liberality of the Temple's squares and recesses are emphasized. Cheerfulness and

---

[5] Lascelles Abercrombie, *Romanticism* (New York: Barnes and Noble, 1963), p. 43.

beneficence characterize the Temple, a most advantageous place, Elia feels, for a man's birthplace. Sentences begin with the word "what," a repetition of form that expresses the mounting wonder experienced by the narrator. "What a cheerful, liberal look," "what a collegiate aspect has that fine Elizabethan hall," and "what an antique air" exhibit a rhetorical pattern that reflects the mounting spirit of excitement and introduces new, prized objects of recollection. The repetition also has the effect of a refrain and carries the narrator and the reader into the magical world of a child's active imagination.

Elia's playfellows, not knowing that he made the fountain in the garden to rise and fall, were almost tempted to "hail the wondrous work as magic" (II, 83). Their active imaginations and strong feelings would have been satisfied almost as easily with a fantastic explanation of the fountain's operation as with a practical one. One of Lamb's enthusiastic observations on the lifegiving quality of Izaac Walton's imagination is applicable to Lamb's evocation of the Temple and its artifacts. In Walton, he writes to Robert Lloyd, "*every thing* is *alive;* the fishes are absolutely *charactered;* and birds and animals are as interesting as men and women."[6] In Lamb, the sundials and fountains are as interesting as the old Benchers. In the square of Lincoln's Inn, "four little winged marble boys used to play their virgin fancies, spouting out ever fresh streams from their innocent-wanton lips" (II, 84). Untroubled, the marble boys spouted out what appeared to the boy Elia a never-ending source of fresh water.

---

[6] *The Letters of Charles Lamb: To Which Are Added Those of His Sister Mary,* ed. E. V. Lucas (London: J. H. Dent; Methuen, 1935), I, 244.

The statues are given life by the child's joyous imagination; his heart invests objects with uncommon meaning. Like the description of the marble effigies in "Blakesmoor in H- - - shire," the description of the marble boys holds contradictory qualities in solution: innocence and sensuousness, stasis and vitality.

Just as the fountain rose and fell mysteriously, so too the rising and the setting of the sun probably seemed wondrous to the boys. Time was not measured mechanically in the garden of the Temple. Time's presence was felt directly; sundials held direct, open correspondence with the source of life and grace. The "almost effaced sun-dials, with their moral inscriptions, seeming coevals with that Time which they measured, and to take their revelations of its flight immediately from heaven," held "correspondence with the fountain of light!" (II, 83). Their suggestion of antiquity made them fit instruments to measure the time that almost stood still in the garden. The child's experience of time, felt as something standing still or moving very slowly, is given expression in Elia's recollections of his efforts to watch the dark line on the sundial. To the watchful eye of a child, time would steal on imperceptibly, "nice as an evanescent cloud" (II, 83).

The sundial taught lessons of temperance in pleasure and moderation in labors. Like Keats's "ditties of no tone,"[7] the sundial spoke silently to the heart. The pretentious sounds of a clock, however, "with its ponderous embowelments of lead and brass, its pert or solemn dulness of communication" (II, 83) are a dead thing compared with "the

---

[7] *The Poetical Works of John Keats,* ed. H. W. Garrod (London: Oxford Univ. Press, 1936), p. 209.

simple altar-like structure, and silent heart-language of the old dial" (II, 83). The sundial combined practical, moral, and aesthetic functions, whereas its modern replacement, the clock, is only useful. "The horologe of the first world," the sundial "was the measure appropriate for sweet plants and flowers to spring by, for the birds to apportion their silver warblings by, for flocks to pasture and be led to fold by" (II, 83). Man and nature move together, harmonizing their activities with the sacred time measured by the sundial. All living things measure their activity by the same time—natural time. In Eden, man with his inventions is not a burden to the rest of life, but, taking his cue from the source of life, he moves in step with the rest of creation. And so the sundial, since it combined so many functions, was a fitting "garden god of Christian gardens" (II, 83), within which a unified sensibility was still possible. Elia uses the same word to describe both the water *fountain* and the "*fountain* of light" (II, 83). Both water and sun are sources of life and power, but the use of the same word to describe water and the sun also suggests that the imagination can see the unity behind all things. The diversity of reality, viewed with the shaping powers of the imagination, will reveal its unity.

Talk of sundials and fountains reminds Elia of Marvell's poem *The Garden*, from which he quotes. The subject of the cited verses is also an integrated universe. Man is at ease in nature; he is not a worry to it. In fact, in Marvell's sweet garden scenes, sensuous delights come to man. Apples drop about his head, grapes crush their wine upon his mouth, and peaches reach themselves into his hands. And yet from these sweet enjoyments the mind

Withdraws into its happiness.
The mind, that ocean, where each kind

Does straight its own resemblance find;
Yet it creates, transcending these,
Far other worlds, and other seas;
Annihilating all that's made
To a green thought in a green shade.[8]

There are, both Lamb and Marvell tell us, garden spots and retreats in reality; but there are also cool, mossy spots in the memory, imperishable because they are preserved in art. The artist delights in building a "fane/In some untrodden region"[9] of his mind.

The fountains of the metropolis, like the sundials, are fast disappearing. *Ubi sunt?* Elia asks. The taste for these things is gone by, he writes:

> and these things are esteemed childish. Why not then gratify children, by letting them stand? Lawyers, I suppose, were children once. They are awakening images to them at least. Why must every thing smack of man, and mannish? Is the world all grown up? Is childhood dead? Or is there not in the bosoms of the wisest and the best some of the child's heart left, to respond to its earliest enchantments?
>
> (II, 84-85)

Lamb, as he does so frequently, is supplying in the course of the essay a reply to Elia's question. Lamb would not have us spend all our days in childhood, but he misses the pleasures of the child's heart, which invested even the most humble objects with life, grace, and beauty. Lamb, as did the other romantics, found in a child's sense of awe, spirit of exaggeration, and willingness to accept mystery characteristics analogous to the activity of the adult imagination. What is a natural and effortless activity for the child must

---

[8] Quoted by Lamb in *Works*, II, 84.
[9] Garrod, p. 212.

be cultivated, however, and constantly nourished in the adult. Like Wordsworth, Lamb found the fountain of renewal in memory.

The inhabitants of the Temple were also an integral part of its enchantments. They are not presented as a mere gallery of portraits; they are given a "local habitation and a name." They shared in the sacredness and awfulness of the Temple, before it became "common and profane" (II, 85). Like the clerks of the South-Sea House, they "partook of the genius of the place" (II, 3). Inextricably bound up with their surroundings, they are perfect complements to the buildings, as if they were growths native to the magnificent, antique place.

Each man was an original. Their uniqueness formed a "sort of Noah's ark" (II, 3), and they reveal as many points of interest as the courts and recesses of the Temple. Elia's descriptions of them are feelingly animated by the impulse of heartfelt memories. The Benchers appealed to and developed a part of the child's imagination. Lamb's imagination maintained an interest in the varied human scene, because as a child he knew such men as the old Benchers. Their irreducible individuality both characterizes and limits them, but they are not caricatures; rather, they are presented in the manner of Hogarth, whose work was so much admired by Lamb. He writes of some of Hogarth's subjects:

> That they bring us acquainted with the everyday human face,— they give us skill to detect those gradations of sense and virtue (which escape the careless or fastidious observer) in the countenances of the world about us; and prevent that disgust at human life, that *taedium quotidianarum formarum*, which an unrestricted passion for ideal forms and beauties is in danger of producing.
> (I, 86)

Marvell and Spenser preside over the first part of the essay, while Lamb recalls his pleasure garden and bower of bliss, whereas Shakespeare, Chaucer, and Hogarth—whose creations (kings, pilgrims, and paupers) have become rooted in our aesthetic consciousness—preside over his description of the Benchers.

Elia begins his portrayals of the old Benchers with gusto, since they are the gods in the pantheon of the Temple and share, like the fountain and sundial, in the enchantment of the place. As did the objects in the garden of the Temple, the Benchers nourished the child's mind; their different characteristics answer to various parts of his imagination. The tone of the portraits varies from awe, terror, and exaggeration (bordering on caricature) in the description of Thomas Coventry, to amusement and humor in the presentation of the pensive Salt, to nostalgia and admiration in the memories of Lovel, and to the playful and gently satiric in the sketches of Barrington, Twopenny, Wharry, and Jackson. Lamb begins, while the powers of imagination and memory are strong, with a description of Coventry, a man of epic stature. His presence and actions soon crowd out the sky. Children fled from him, as they would have from an Elisha bear:

His [Coventry's] growl was as thunder in their ears, whether he spake to them in mirth or in rebuke, his invitatory notes being, indeed, of all, the most repulsive and horrid. Clouds of snuff, aggravating the natural terrors of his speech, broke from each majestic nostril, darkening the air. He took it, not by pinches, but a palmful at once, diving for it under the mighty flaps of his old-fashioned waistcoat pocket; his waistcoat red and angry, his coat dark rappee, tinctured by dye original, and by adjuncts, with buttons of obsolete gold. And so he paced the terrace.

(II, 85)

The child's strong feelings are reflected in the vivid description of Coventry's manner and his clothes. Each observation of his habits, speech, physical appearance, mannerisms, and gestures reflects part of his character, as it is remembered by Elia. The Bencher's prepossessing appearance, his undeviating manner of walking, his opinions, his humor, and his thorough miserliness—all contribute to the sense of an organic creation. Coventry is not the sum of a number of details linked together lifelessly, since the child's intense feelings invest each part of his character with significance. The exaggerated language is not merely quaint; it reflects the child's view of Coventry.

Samuel Salt, a milder man than Coventry, frequently accompanied him in walks on the terrace of the Temple. Of major interest in the description of Salt is the difference between his public and his private person. Salt was not an awesome figure, as was Coventry, and their differences of character are reflected in Elia's description of them. Whereas a spirit of exaggeration informs the description of Coventry, Elia does not hesitate to mention Salt's shortcomings, illustrated by humorous anecdotes. Although a shy man of unprepossessing intelligence, with a habit of speaking unseasonably, he enjoyed a reputation as a man of application and as a person fit to be consulted on numerous matters, because of the "mere trick of gravity" (II, 86) and the natural genius of his factotum, Lovel. Coventry and Salt are opposites:

They were coevals, and had nothing but that and their benchship in common. In politics Salt was a whig, and Coventry a staunch tory. Many a sarcastic growl did the latter cast out— for Coventry had a rough spinous humour—at the political confederates of his associate, which rebounded from the gentle bosom of the latter like cannon-balls from wool. You could not ruffle Samuel Salt.

(II, 85-86)

Lamb does not present the portraits as set cameo pieces; rather, he develops the characters throughout the essay. The comparisons drawn between the two Benchers, Coventry and Salt, provide links from one characterization to another and heighten the qualities of each. Coventry is independent, blustering, and awesome; Salt is dependent, unassuming, and indolent. By comparing their qualities Elia increases Coventry's industry and Salt's indolence, and he varies the method of presenting them. Coventry's miserliness was well known, yet "by taking care of the pence, he is often enabled to part with the pounds, upon a scale that leaves us careless generous fellows halting at an immeasurable distance behind" (II, 87). Salt is no sluggard about his indolence: "Lovel took care of everything. He was at once his clerk, his good servant, his dresser, his friend, his 'flapper,' his guide, stopwatch, auditor, treasurer" (II, 87). Coventry made things happen, whereas things happened to Salt.

Lovel, full of rogueries and inventions, "by the dint of natural genius merely" (II, 88), made cribbage boards and cabinet toys to perfection, played equally well at quadrille or bowls, and made punch better than most men of his rank. All his actions reflect his naturalness and frank manner. He was a "man of incorrigible and lasting honesty," who "once wrested a sword out of the hand of a man of quality that had drawn upon him; and pommelled him severely with the hilt of it. The swordsman had offered insult to a female—an occasion upon which no odds against him could have prevented the interference of Lovel" (II, 88).

Although some of the Benchers, such as Coventry, Salt, and Lovel, are described at length, a number are given several sentences only. Daines Barrington

> walked burly and square—in imitation, I think, of Coventry—howbeit he attained not to the dignity of his prototype. Nevertheless, he did pretty well, upon the strength of being a tolerable antiquarian, and having a brother a bishop. When the account of his year's treasurership came to be audited, the following singular charge was unanimously disallowed by the bench: 'Item, disbursed Mr. Allen, the gardener, twenty shillings, for stuff to poison the sparrows, by my orders.'
>
> (II, 89)

Barrington does not appear spiteful, but there is something peevish about a man who would poison birds. But his efforts to rid the Temple of sparrows is not surprising, since much of his life is something of a negation. He tries to imitate Coventry, is only a tolerable antiquarian, and gains some recognition as the brother of a bishop. He lives off others, and he is probably a little jealous of anything that shows spirit and life. A mannerism or habit catches irrevocably some of the Benchers. Wharry, whose features were lean and spiteful, "would pinch his cat's ears extremely when anything offended him" (II, 87). Mingay had an iron right hand, which became emblematic of power for the child, and so Elia received hints of allegory from men as well as from such objects as winged horses or frescoes.

When Elia nears the end of his recollections of the Benchers, his memories of them become halting and eventually trail off. As memory and imagination fail him, the portraits become shorter, until he concludes his recollections of the Benchers with a one-sentence description of Baron Maseres, who walked in the costume of the period of George the Second. Earlier in the essay Elia had lamented the passing of fountains and sundials; now, at the end of his recollections of old Benchers, he wonders where they have gone. Were they, he asks, merely the creations of a child's active imagination and sense of exaggeration? He regrets the passing of that power in his childhood that gave such significance to the Benchers, who made up the mythology of the Temple. His account of them, he feels, fails to measure up to what he thought they must have appeared to him when a child. The clear light of reason has dried up the preternatural mist that enshrouded them. But Elia believes that

> in the heart of childhood, there will, for ever, spring up a well of innocent or wholesome superstition—the seed of exaggeration will be busy there, and vital—from every-day forms educing the unknown and the uncommon. In that little Goshen there will be light, when the grown world flounders about in the darkness of sense and materiality. While childhood, and while dreams, reducing childhood, shall be left, imagination shall not have spread her holy wings totally to fly the earth.
>
> (II, 90)

And, Elia might have added, while the fount of memory remains to animate the imagination. Lamb, of course, believes that memories will energize the adult mind and enable it to create little Goshens. We have seen, in fact, the imagination using the seeds of memory to invest common objects with significance and to lighten up the world of sense and materiality. The memories of childhood provide materials for the imagination and warm it to its task.

In the postscript to the essay Elia corrects an error made with regard to Samuel Salt. Salt was not, as Elia had written, a bachelor, since he had been married but had lost his wife in childbirth. It seems odd that Elia should bother to correct a mistake that could easily have been made without the reader's knowledge. Lamb knew that the choice of materials from contemporary or near contemporary men would pose difficulties for him as an artist, since many readers would read to judge the accuracy of the portraits against what they thought were the originals. What is important about the choice of real names and places, however, is not that they can be verified, but that they give the illusion of reality. The Benchers, streets, buildings, and actual London settings are important because they have been hallowed by memories and the imagination. Though the Benchers are rooted in reality, "their importance is from the past" (II, 7). The "holiness of the Heart's affections"[10] has cast an animating hue and an ennobling mist over them.

Evidently troubled by readers who were more interested in art conforming to reality than in art creating an illusion of reality, Lamb decided to clarify his intentions in the essays. Having admitted his error with regard to Salt to the reader, Elia warns us: "Henceforth let no one receive the narratives of Elia for true records! They are, in truth, but shadows of fact—verisimilitudes, not verities—or sitting but upon the remote edges and outskirts of history" (II, 90). Elia reminds his readers that his intentions are not those of the older magazines, such as the *Gentleman's*. Elia's essays are "verisimilitudes, not verities." By turning memory into art, Lamb has demonstrated both the source of his materials and the history of the growth of his mind.

Benchers and South Sea Clerks, not solitaries, wandering soldiers, or lonely shepherds, are the human figures in his landscapes. They share, as do Wordsworth's solitaries, in the genius of the place, but the spirit of the place is urban and

---

[10] *The Letters of John Keats 1814-1821*, ed. Hyder E. Rollins (Cambridge, Mass.: Harvard Univ. Press, 1958), I, 184.

social. Lamb describes many men whose lives are bound up in one another's, whether the setting is Christ's Hospital, Mackery End, the South-Sea House, or the Temple. Lamb finds the materials and symbols for his art in man and man's dwellings rather than in nature.

# III

## COMPLEMENTARY MODES OF EXPERIENCE

*"Mrs. Battle's Opinions on Whist"*
*"Mackery End, in Hertfordshire"*

I HOPED to demonstrate in the last chapter that Lamb frequently uses setting, objects, and narrative to shape and unify the activity of the imagination. He employs a similar method in "Mrs. Battle's Opinions on Whist" and "Mackery End, in Hertfordshire," but he uses the device of the character to control and unify his numerous, related themes. Whereas setting and narrative incarnate Lamb's process of thought in "The Old Benchers of the Inner Temple," description of the inner life of Elia, his cousin Bridget, and Sarah Battle shapes the activity of Lamb's imagination in these two essays. Sarah Battle, Elia, and Bridget are among Lamb's most memorable creations, but their opinions and habits of life suggest meanings that go beyond their persons. Homely matter, drawn from their experience, provides an analogy for more ambitious concerns.

For example, although Elia's description of Sarah Battle is limited to some remarks that she had made to him about cards, Lamb explores the implications of her opinions so skillfully that she reveals her essential character to us. His method is to describe her views of various card games, such as whist, piquet, cribbage, and ombre, in such a manner that her opinions reflect her fundamental assumptions about the nature of art, of man, and of the universe. Furthermore, her opinions echo conceptions and principles commonly accepted by men of the eighteenth century. Finally, the description of Mrs. Battle's opinions provides a vehicle for subtle references to the differences between imaginative and ethical and practical modes of consciousness. Yet Lamb's art achieves these thematic concerns without sacrificing interest in the character of Mrs. Battle. An old woman's opinions on cards hardly seem a promising subject for an essay, but it is a tribute to Lamb's genius that these humble materials generate ever-widening circles of interest.

To some extent "Mrs. Battle's Opinions on Whist" can be read as an inquiry into the meaning of the word "play" for Elia and for Mrs. Battle. In the mind of the latter play is associated, perhaps even synonymous, with work, duty, and the battle for salvation.[1] For Elia play comes to mean recreation and a spirit of idleness that contributes to the renewal of the human spirit. Sarah Battle loved to play cards: "A clear fire, a clean hearth, and the rigour of the game" was her

---

[1] Donald H. Reiman's excellent discussion of "Mrs. Battle's Opinions" in his article, "Thematic Unity in Lamb's Familiar Essays," *JEGP*, 64 (1965), 470-478, has been helpful on several points.

"celebrated wish."[2] Clarity, cleanliness, and manly vigor are high in her hierarchy of values and suggest a mind that puts cleanliness next to godliness. Her religious devotions and her whist game are inextricably associated in her mind, so that her remarks on cards reflect her deepest moral convictions. Her judgments of card games and of those differing with her opinions on whist reflect a complex set of moral, practical, and social standards.

Whatever Sarah Battle does, she does with conviction and determination. Her judgments and opinions tend to be absolute; there is no room for compromise, ambiguity, or indecision. Those who would dally at games, for example, are suspect. She detests triflers at cards, who play indifferently, not caring whether they win or lose, or even whether they play at all. As her name suggests, she was "none of your lukewarm gamesters" (II, 32); she played cards as if she kept before her Christ's warning to the lukewarm that he would spit them out of his mouth. Players who approach the table without a proper sense of devotion to the game are insufferable and no better than flies. Sarah Battle would rarely join them in a game:

She loved a thorough-paced partner, a determined enemy. She took, and gave, no concessions. She hated favours. She never made a revoke, nor ever passed it over in her adversary without exacting the utmost forfeiture. She fought a good fight: cut and thrust. She held not her good sword (her cards) "like a dancer." She sate bolt upright; and neither showed you her cards, nor desired to see yours.

(II, 32-33)

---

[2] *The Works of Charles and Mary Lamb,* ed. E. V. Lucas (London: Methuen, 1903-5), II, 32. Volume number and page numbers for subsequent quotations from the *Works* will be given in the text.

Every detail of Elia's description contributes to the presentation of Sarah Battle and her opinions. Her appearance, her language, and her views reflect each other. Although her opinions are given us through the voice of Elia, he identifies himself with her and employs the diction, the metaphors, and the rhetorical patterns that she would use if she were speaking for herself. Forceful, vivid verbs are used to describe her feelings and are central to the meaning of her person; she is a woman of action and strong character. The pronoun "she" begins the sentences and enforces our impression of her as an indomitable spirit. Sarah Battle is morally and physically upright and would settle only for first place in any endeavor. The persistent sentence pattern accommodates itself to her attitudes. The sentences are curt and to the point; there are no nuances, overtones, or mysteries. Her likes and dislikes in cards are described in martial metaphors. Cards, as is all of life, are warfare for Mrs. Battle, a true Christian warrior.

Although she is an exacting woman, both in her devotions and in her play, Mrs. Battle, like other people, has her superstitions. Elia "had heard her declare, under the rose, that Hearts was her favorite suit" (II, 33). Mention of this detail adds a dimension to her character, since one would not expect a woman of Mrs. Battle's firmness of character to choose hearts for her favorite suit. That her choice of suit appealed to her blind side is evident when we remember that the heart is considered the seat of the affections, sentiment, silliness, and the passions—all of which are distrusted by the sober-minded Mrs. Battle.

She never interrupted her game for anything, and miscellaneous conversation was forbidden at her table. Her emphatic reminder to triflers at the game that "cards were cards" is ironic, since cards are not merely cards for Sarah Battle but a skirmish in the battle for salvation. In her system of values a book is a trifling recreation over which she unbends her mind after the labor of the game. Since in the Puritan ethic cards would be an idle diversion, fraught with perils for the ever-vigilant Christian soldier, Mrs. Battle redeems her pleasure by making it work; cards "was her business, her duty, the thing she came into the world to do" (II, 33). Her opinions about whist ultimately reflect the rigors of moral battles. She brings the same set of attitudes and moral fervor to both her devotions and her card playing.

Mrs. Battle's observations on ombre, quadrille, cribbage, piquet, and the features of cards further develop her character and expand the implications of two contrasting clusters of association. Rationality, solidity, and constancy characterize her likes. Whatever she dislikes is called trifling, indifferent, miscellaneous, and, we suspect, immoral.

Pope is her favorite author and the sprightliest of his works, *The Rape of the Lock,* is her favorite poem. Her major interest in the poem, however, is the game of ombre, which she once played over with Elia, pointing out how it agrees with and differs from quadrille. The game of quadrille was her first love but gave way, in her maturer esteem, to whist:

> The former, she said, was showy and specious, and likely to allure young persons. The uncertainty and quick shifting of partners— a thing which the constancy of whist abhors;—the dazzling supremacy and regal investiture of Spadille—absurd, as she justly observed, in the pure aristocrasy of whist, where his crown and garter give him no proper power above his brother-nobility of the Aces;—the giddy vanity, so taking to the inexperienced, of playing alone:—above all, the overpowering attractions of a *Sans Prendre Vole,*—to the triumph of which there is certainly nothing parallel or approaching, in the contingencies of whist;—all

these, she would say, make quadrille a game of captivation to the young and enthusiastic. But whist was the *solider* game: that was her word. It was a long meal; not, like quadrille, a feast of snatches.

(II, 33)

Elia's references to various areas of human experience, such as wars, politics, appetites, and religion, give density and range to the essay. They are knit together by a number of covert assumptions.

Mrs. Battle's appearance reminds Elia of an eighteenth-century grand dame: he refers to her "fine last-century countenance" (II, 33). Her opinions are also of that century. In the description of her judgments and feelings there are faint echoes of Newton, Descartes, and Locke. She has an empirical mind that values and emphasizes order, constancy, clear and distinct ideas. As in previous descriptions of her judgments, patterns of meaning gather around her likes and dislikes. "Showy," "specious," "uncertainty," "dazzling," "giddy," "enthusiastic," and "shifting" are contrasted with "sober," "mature," "constancy," in short, *"solider."*

Where propriety, decorum, and a sense of restraint are lacking, there is cause, in Mrs. Battle's mind, for suspicion, possibly even grounds for moral disapproval. She likes a hierarchical order, a chain of being, within which each thing has its place, and she considers any deviation from the norm an aberration. And so the "pure aristocracy of whist" is preferred to some of the more alluring but less solid games. Mrs. Battle argues for the retention of the rank of cards and is probably a proponent of political aristocracy.

Her opinions on quadrille and whist reflect her like of the ordered, the rational, and the substantial:

The skirmishes of quadrille, she would say, reminded her of the petty ephemeral embroilments of the little Italian states, depicted by Machieavel; perpetually changing postures and connexions; bitter foes to-day, sugared darlings to-morrow; kissing and scratching in a breath;—but the wars of whist were comparable to the long, steady, deep-rooted, rational, antipathies of the great French and English nations.

(II, 34)

Martial imagery still forms the basis of her description. That the skirmishes of quadrille are irrational is sufficient grounds for dismissing them. The rhythm of the sentence changes with the contrasted opinions: quick, brisk, broken phrases lengthen out as the description turns to the substantial French and British wars. Metaphors and similes taken from eating, social relationships, and international wars reflect her basic assumptions about the universe that reflect in their turn principles of the eighteenth century. Her opinions about whist are a microcosmic representation of a set of values, political, moral, and aesthetic.

Mrs. Battle would have considered her dislike of superficiality in anything a virtue and so she brought to cards and literature the same set of values that she brought to the management of her life. Qualities of character and judgment that would be acceptable in situations demanding moral judgment are ruinous, however, when applied to games. Cribbage, when judged by the rules of whist, is found lacking. Any deviation from the rules of cards—that is, the rules of whist—is abhorred as a superfluity and considered a violation of the conventional rules. Cribbage she called a vulgar and an ungrammatical game; a formalist in her moral habits, she is also a formalist in her use of the language. She could not bring herself to say "Go" or to take nobs by declaring "two for his heels" (II, 35).

Elia considers Mrs. Battle's self-denial extremely genteel; it is in fact a stifling fastidiousness and a rigorous application of rules and prescriptions to games and language.
Piquet, although she thinks that it is the better game than
cribbage for two persons, also merits her disfavor, because
the terms such as piquet, repique, and capot savored of
pedantry and affectation. Like the Caledonians, Mrs. Battle
eschewed any type of individuality, although she herself was
a unique person.

Sarah Battle is literal minded. Her objections to flushes
in cribbage are based on her unswerving opinions of what
she thinks cards really are: "That any one should claim four
by virtue of holding cards of the same mark and colour,
without reference to the playing of the game, or the individual worth of pretentions of the cards themselves!" (II, 34).
She held flushes an irrational intrusion into the game and "as
pitiful an ambition at cards as alliteration is in authorship"
(II, 34). She considers the delights of literature ornaments
and decorations exterior to the essential business of writing.

Lamb's juxtaposition of cards and writing in Mrs. Battle's mind is not accidental. Those who approach recreation,
and Lamb would include literature among recreations, with
moral and practical preconceptions are likely to dismiss many
of a writer's achievements with the tools of his craft as
pleasant but unessential additions to the real business of literature. For many men of the age of the enlightenment matter was separable from and more important than form. The
utilitarians of the Victorian period were to equate the
pleasures of pushpins with the delights of literature.

Mrs. Battle's favorite game was whist, since she believed that in square or quadrate games all that can be at-
tained in card-playing is accomplished. In her description of

the advantages of whist, art and morality become inter-
changeably fused. All the qualities that characterize the real
world are found in whist, according to Sarah Battle's account. In whist, judgments are to be made, superfluities to be
avoided, and gains to be considered. She would retain only
the utilitarian aspects of cards, reducing games to the point
where they resemble the real world of practical concerns and
moral judgments. Goals, decisions, alliances, and "the incen-
tives of profit with honor" (II, 36) are among the advantages
of whist. Play imitates life so closely there is no difference
between the two. Spectators are not required in whist nor is
their sympathy needed, since there is no make-believe: all is
real. Whist demands judgment and "abhors neutrality, or
interests beyond its sphere" (II, 36). But it is a spirit of neutrality and the freedom to breathe beyond the confines of
the conscience and the will that Elia seeks in games.

Even the excitement of a game of chance would be
nothing, Mrs. Battle believed, without some stake. Where
would be the glory? But where chance was an element in any
game, she refused to play without stakes. Chance became
something only when something else depended on it, and
that something else could not be glory. Submissions to
chance, unless there was some end or money involved, were
distasteful to her. She would control and understand all the
aspects of her life. Yet games that depended solely on each
individual's skills were also not to her taste. When played for
money, these games were merely a means of taking advantage; if played without a stake, for glory, they only pitted one
man's wit against another's and so she demanded chance as
well as a stake in games.

Mrs. Battle even wished that whist were more gravely
simple than it was, and, in Elia's mind "would have stripped

it of some appendages, which, in the state of human frailty, may be venially, and even commendably, allowed of" (II, 34). She would have, for example, had one suit always trumps and retained only one of the two colors of cards. Fripperies, little pleasures, and the delights of the senses have no reason to exist in her scheme of things. Elia suggests that they be allowed man, even if—and he says this slyly—they be venially sinful. Mrs. Battle would strip not only cards but also the world of individuality, mystery, and spontaneity. Her moral sense tends to regard all decisions as a choice between absolutes; her aesthetic sense leads her to desensualize objects and to dehumanize man. She falls victim to the world of abstractions. Elia agrees with Mrs. Battle that the game of cards would go on very well without all its colorful delights, but, he says, "the *beauty* of cards would be extinguished for ever" (II, 34-35). Man, he reminds her, is a creature of senses as well as of reason and enjoys having his senses appealed to. He asks her to imagine

> a dull deal board, or drum head, to spread them [cards] on, instead of that nice verdant carpet (next to nature's), fittest arena for those courtly combatants to play their gallant jousts and turneys in!—Exchange those delicately-turned ivory markers—(work of Chinese artist, unconscious of their symbol,—or as profanely slighting their true application as the arrantest Ephesian journeyman that turned out those little shrines for the goddess)— exchange them for little bits of leather (our ancestors' money) or chalk and a slate!
>
> (II, 35)

All the trappings and ornaments of cards, which Mrs. Battle would call superfluous, although they have no utilitarian usefulness, add to the beauty and the imaginative appeal of the game. Although Elia uses, like Mrs. Battle, martial imagery to defend the colors of suits, the ornamental pegs on a cribbage board, and the various pictures on cards, he substitutes jousts and tourneys for battles and skirmishes. He conjures up a picure of Merry England. Elia argues that by judging all of man's actions, his achievements, his pleasures, and his art according to ethical and practical standards, we would dismiss much of our experience as irrelevant and perhaps even as morally reprehensible. The Chinese and Ephesian artists work to create beautiful objects, and they are slightly, if at all, aware of any practical use the "ivory markers" and "little shrines" may have.

Mrs. Battle admits the soundness of Elia's arguments, and it is to her approval of his point of view that he attributes his legacy from the old lady, "a curious cribbage board, made of the finest Sienna marble . . . and a trifle of five hundred pounds" (II, 35). The gifts enforce the comparison made so far between the practical and the imaginative. Her concessions to Elia are revealed in her legacy, since she did not enjoy cribbage. Although the cribbage board will help players to keep score, it will also give pleasure to Elia as a finely crafted work of art. Yet she also gives him money to remind Elia that, although she might have seen the truth of his disagreement with her, she would still insist on the value of common sense and the spirit of practicality. Despite Elia's reference he could hardly have considered the five hundred pounds a trifle, especially when we remember that he was a "lean annuitant" (II, 1).

Practical considerations determine her defense of cards against those who object to the game because it fosters bad passions. She retorts:

> Man is a gaming animal. He must be always trying to get the better in something or other:—that this passion can scarcely be more

safely expended than upon a game at cards: that cards are a temporary illusion; in truth, a mere drama; for we do but *play* at being mightily concerned, where a few idle shillings are at stake, yet, during the illusion, we *are* as mightily concerned as those whose stake is crowns and kingdoms. They are a sort of dreamfighting; much ado; great battling, and little bloodshed; mighty means for disproportioned ends; quite as diverting, and a great deal more innoxious, than many of those more serious *games* of life, which men play, without esteeming them to be such.—

(II, 37)

Although her observations on man's gambling nature and instinct may be sound—does she not sound like Hobbes? —her views obliterate the distinction between art and morality, if they are imposed on an aesthetic theory. Mrs. Battle appears to understand the essential nature of play and of the aesthetic experience—that they are an experience of an illusion—but she demands of the illusion that it faithfully mirror reality and common life. She sees the elements in a game gratifying some principle in our nature; card games dissipate hostile feelings and aggressive instincts. Playing at cards is a harmless way to act out our passions, since we can play at reality without the sometimes brutal consequences of real actions. Card games appear little different from the more serious games of life, other than that they appear to have no serious consequences. The real world and Mrs. Battle's world of illusion are interchangeable.

Elia deferentially disagrees with Mrs. Battle's opinions and slyly says there have been occasions in his life when "playing at cards *for nothing* has even been agreeable. When I am in sickness, or not in the best spirits, I sometimes call for the cards, and play a game at piquet *for love* with my cousin Bridget—Bridget Elia" (II, 37). He plays simply to enjoy himself, not to gain honor or glory. Although he humbly admits that enjoyment and the desire to idle away a few moments in pleasure are inferior springs of action, he suggests "there is such a thing in nature . . . as *sick whist*" (II, 37). When a man is not feeling well, he is not greatly concerned with means and ends, losses and gains; rather, he would forget for a moment his discomforts. And is not Lamb suggesting a humble analogy for the experience of the imagination?

Elia recalls that last game he had with his cousin:

(I capotted her)—(dare I tell thee, how foolish I am?)—I wished it might have lasted for ever, though we gained nothing, and lost nothing, though it was a mere shade of play: I would be content to go on in that idle folly for ever. The pipkin should be ever boiling, that was to prepare the gentle lenitive to my foot, which Bridget was doomed to apply after the game was over: and, as I do not much relish appliances, there it should ever bubble. Bridget and I should be ever playing.

(II, 37)

Humble motives, little pleasures, and a homely setting are associated with the Elias' game and are contrasted with the mightly efforts of Mrs. Battle in her drawing room. Although both are types of play and illusion, Mrs. Battle's game of whist and Elia's game of piquet with Bridget reflect two different conceptions of the aesthetic experience. Elia's choice of what appear depreciatory phrases to describe their game—"a mere shade of play" and "idle folly"—are, in fact, complimentary words. In the world of Lamb's imagination Elia and Bridget would ever be playing under the illusion that they are in a timeless world, wherein they are liberated from the cares and rigors of the will and the moral judgment. Although their game had little relation to the real world of actions and decisions, Elia could have played at it forever.

Lamb is suggesting the playful nature of the aesthetic experience and the imagination. He associates playing and games with the activity of the imagination to illustrate its affinities with make-believe and recreation. Life can be experienced in play and by the imagination without our having to judge the activity. And both playing and the experience of the imagination do not demand or expect results other than enjoyment and, on the higher levels of the imagination, the liberation of the human spirit from the world of time, of the will, and of the conscience.

The choice of cards as the main matter for the essay reflects its concerns. Cards have both a practical and an aesthetic value, and so Lamb's themes are inherent in the objects of the essay. Cards provide the materials for the essay and give unity to the activity of the imagination.

Lamb uses the method of "Mrs. Battle" in "Mackery End, in Hertfordshire." Elia begins the essay with a statement of fact, a type of opening already familiar to us. He writes: "Bridget Elia has been my housekeeper for many a long year. I have obligations to Bridget, extending beyond the period of memory" (II, 75). "Many a long year" suggests both the length and fullness of each year of their lives together and Elia's awareness that he can still recover their time together through the memory. His obligations to Bridget as a housekeeper are of considerable importance in the management of his daily affairs, since Elia shows little talent for practical considerations. His debts to her and their different habits of mind and of living form the greater part of the first half of the essay. The second half, describing their visit to Mackery End, considers his obligations to her, "extending beyond the period of memory."

Bridget's and Elia's domestic arrangements are rarely marred by bickerings; in fact, their different habits complement each other so well that they live together in "a sort of double singleness" (II, 75). Elia's life with Bridget is comfortable, and he feels there is no reason to regret his decision not to marry. Their complete knowledge of each other's habits and personality creates a sense of ease and is a source of pleasure in their relationship. Their familiarity with each other is of that sort found only between people who have known each other and shared their lives together for a long time. Bridget, particularly, relies on the comforts of familiarity and on the assurances that her knowledge and expectations of Elia are rarely contradicted. On one occasion, Elia writes, "upon my dissembling a tone in my voice more kind than ordinary, my cousin burst into tears, and complained that I was altered" (II, 75).

This desire to have reality meet her expectations of it carries over into her reading habits. Her choice of reading materials reflects her own understanding and knowledge of the world; she is engaged by the perpetual replaying of reality. Nothing "out of the road of common sympathy" has any appeal for Bridget; she has a "native disrelish of anything that sounds odd or bizarre" (II, 75). That art should imitate nature—that is, the external world of actions—is high on her list of requirements for successful fiction, since she "holds Nature more clever" (II, 75). She appears to represent the reader of Lamb's day about whom he complained that they were spoiled by the fiction of common life, so that they brought all their moral and practical preconceptions to their reading of literature.

Bridget is pleased, much more than Elia, with a reflection of common life in literature:

While I [Elia writes] am hanging over (for the thousandth time) some passage in old Burton, or one of his strange contemporaries, she is abstracted in some modern tale, or adventure, whereof our common reading-table is daily fed with assiduously fresh supplies. Narrative teases me. I have little concern in the progress of events. She must have a story—well, ill or indifferently told—so there be life stirring in it, and plenty of good or evil accidents. The fluctuations of fortune in fiction—and almost in real life—have ceased to interest, or operate but dully upon me. Out-of-the-way humours and opinions—heads with some diverting twist in them—the oddities of authorship please me most.

(II, 75)

The difference in meaning between "hanging over" and "abstracted" points up the difference between their reading habits. Elia delights in the drama of the mind, whereas Bridget enjoys reading literature that imitates actions. Since Elia returns to his favorites so often, we can assume that he does not exhaust either the contents of the books or what his imagination brings to them. He is not a reader mindlessly entering a book to escape, but a creative and an idle reader; he reads to enjoy and to recreate his mind, not to sharpen his judgment or to acquire information. Bridget, on the other hand, loses herself in modern tales or adventure stories that provide excitement and action. She is evidently a voracious reader, who devours books to be entertained, since her supplies must be replenished daily. She must have a narrative that gives the illusion of mirroring life. Narrative assumes a beginning, a middle, and an end; the rise and fall of actions; the illusion of time passing; deeds and consequences; and causes and effects. It appears, then, that Bridget is most pleased with fiction that strives to create and to imitate the pattern and rhythm of the exterior world of actions, whereas Elia is interested both in the interior life of the author of his reading matter and in his imaginative response to the drama of another mind.

Sidelights and excursions into the "oddities of authorship" please Elia most, and so he has little interest in reading a literature that is only a reenactment of outer reality. His interests lie in those books that do not demand any narrative sequence to maintain his interest. He reads authors, such as Burton or the "somewhat fantastical, and original-brain'd, generous Margaret Newcastle" (II, 76), writers who appear to have no application to the practical affairs of daily life. Variety, the odd, the bizarre, originality, and nobility of conception are the qualities that Elia holds dear and expects of his favorites.

It seems ironic, then, that Elia, while continuing his description of Bridget, should mention his regret at her too frequent association with "free-thinkers—leaders, and disciples, of novel philosophies and systems" (II, 76). Although he has expressed an interest in the odd or irregular, he does not relish their presence. He is not contradicting himself; rather, Elia is distinguishing real individuality of spirit and true creative genius from the foppery and evanescence of novelty. Although Bridget is frequently in their company, she neither argues with nor accepts the opinions of the creators of new systems of thought. Her security in the familiar and enjoyment of the common extends to her choice of friends and ideas. Virtues and the moral sense inculcated in her during childhood still retain their authority over her mind. Elia is indirectly reminding us that, though Bridget reads contemporary fiction, she is not an addlebrain who is constantly shifting her opinions. Her continuous acceptance of the good and the venerable of her childhood reflects her

tendency to rely on the familiar and her apparent unwillingness to test new ideas.

It also seems strange that Elia, who professes a strong
interest in the past and little interest in the accidents of real
life, observes that in disputes between himself and Bridget
he generally is "right in matters of fact, dates, and circumstances," and that his cousin is right "upon moral points;
upon something proper to be done, or let alone" (II, 76). The
areas of success of each one, however, are consonant with
their habits of mind as Elia has presented them. Elia is right
in matters that are concrete and specific: we see, for example, how carefully he locates Mackery End and gives the
time of their arrival there. Bridget, however, relying on her
childhood principles and her knowledge of actions derived
from her reading, is generally right on matters that call for
the will and the conscience.

Elia mentions several of Bridget's foibles that slightly
irritate him. "Her presence of mind," Elia writes, "is equal to
the most pressing trials of life, but will sometimes desert her
on trifling occasions. When the purpose requires it, and is a
thing of moment, she can speak to it greatly; but in matters
which are not stuff of the conscience, she hath been known
sometimes to let slip a word less seasonably" (II, 76). Bridget
appears to have some of Sarah Battle's moral vigor and spirit
of absolutism. Se answers yes or no, without fully understanding the meaning of the question; she is generally right
about moral points; and her presence of mind rarely deserts
her in matters of conscience.

In a period of stress she is a welcome comfort, "but in
the teazing accidents, and minor perplexities, which do not
call out the *will* to meet them, she sometimes maketh matters
worse by an excess of participation" (II, 77). Ironically, it is

Bridget in the Elia household who is practical, able to face crises, and a buffer against the major distresses of life. Elia, on the other hand, pursues his "out-of-the-way humours and opinions," reacts to the "beautiful obliquities" (II, 76) of seventeenth-century prose, and has the patience to submit himself to the mysteries of life. If the reader is inclined to prefer either Bridget or Elia, he should keep in mind Elia's earlier description of their domestic arrangement as "a sort of double singleness." Bridget and Elia represent complementary modes of experience: the practical and the imaginative. Their habits and ways of life are not antagonistic, since the characteristics of each cousin are valuable in different areas of experience. In the best of his art Lamb recognizes the claims of both art and reality, of both the practical and the imaginative. Lamb seems to have projected his experience into Elia and Bridget so as to better understand his thoughts about man's various faculties, such as imagination, will, conscience, and memory.

Mention of what a pleasant companion Bridget is on journeys reminds Elia of a trip that they had made several summers before into Hertfordshire. A farmhouse there, called Mackery End, is the scene of Elia's oldest memory. He had visited the place when he was a child under the care of Bridget, but he can barely remember his first visit there. Bridget and Elia set out on their second visit, some forty years after their first, uncertain whether they will find relatives or strangers living at Mackery End. Their different pleasures and individual reactions to the scene confirm Elia's description of their life as a "sort of double singleness." Any anxiety Elia had about the success of his visit was eased at first sight of the old farmhouse. Although every trace of it was effaced from his recollections, sight of the place gave

Elia a greater pleasure than any he had experienced for years. Elia had no memories of his own to compete with the sight of the farmhouse. Bridget, however, had shared, over the years, her memories of their first visit to Mackery End with Elia, and so he does have "obligations to Bridget, extending beyond the period of memory."

Bridget is a link to Elia's distant past, kept alive for him by her memory. For, Elia tells us, though he had forgotten the spot, "*we* had never forgotten being there together, and we had been talking about Mackery End all our lives, till memory on my part became mocked with a phantom of itself, and I thought I knew the aspect of a place, which, when present, O how unlike it was to *that*, which I had conjured up so many times instead of it!" (II, 77). Without Bridget's memories that part of his past would have been forgotten, depriving him not only of knowledge about himself but also of the materials that became part of his "phantom" creation of Mackery End.

Bridget's memories are shaped by Elia's imagination, until they became as real and vivid as if they were his own memories. Elia's pleasure is doubled, however, both because reality did not disappoint him, and because the scene did not compete with or destroy his conception of Mackery End. His pleasure was increased by the surprise that, although Mackery End actually was unlike his fair creation, yet it was equal to it:

> Still the air breathed balmily about it; the season was in the "heart of June," and I could say with the poet,

But thou, that didst appear so fair
    To fond imagination,
Dost rival in the light of day
    Her delicate creation![3]

(II, 77)

Reality was as pleasurable as the imaginative creation. Mackery End was as fair and as pleasant as sweet dreams and delicate imaginings.

Bridget's pleasure at first was so great that she too was overcome by the beauty of the scene, but hers was "more a waking bliss" (II, 77) than Elia's. Unlike Elia, Bridget easily remembered the old farmhouse and was a little upset with some of the altered features. Her pleasure lay in recognizing the place and refamiliarizing herself with the farm: "The scene soon re-confirmed itself in her affections—and she traversed every out-post of the old mansion, to the wood-house, the orchard, the place where the pigeon-house had stood (house and birds were alike flown)—with a breathless impatience of recognition" (II, 78). Bridget enjoyed adjusting and comparing her present experience with her memories of Mackery End: her expectations and anticipations are realized.

Elia relies on his cousin to get them into the house, since he is terribly shy in introducing himself to strangers or scarcely remembered kinsfolk. Having no such scruples, Bridget enters the house alone and soon returns with "a creature that might have sat to a sculptor for the image of Welcome" (II, 78). Just as any anxious curiosity about the place had been immediately dispelled upon sight of the farm, so

---

[3] Lamb quotes from Wordsworth's "Yarrow Visited."

too Elia's hesitancy in approaching the house was unwar-
ranted. Kinsfolk still occupied the mansion, since the young-
est of the Gladmans, who by marriage became a Burton, was
mistress of the house. This cousin had no memory of Elia and
only a dim recollection of Bridget. In the genial atmosphere
of Hertfordshire, however, ties of kinship provided the basis
for quick friendships and warm exchanges. Love and fond
imagination enhance and sanctify Elia's recollections of
their reception. In his memory Hertfordshire becomes the
promised land of milk and honey; the three graces, tranquillity, beneficience, and hospitality, reign there. The Elias'
reception by husband and wife was graceful and loving and
rivals the fair creations of art. After dining on "the fatted
calf" (II, 78), already prepared as if in anticipation of their
coming, they went with their cousin to nearby Wheathamp-
stead to meet her mother and older sisters.

The kindness of their reception by the Gladmans
warmed Bridget's memory into a "thousand half-obliterated
recollections of things and persons . . . old effaced images of
more than half-forgotten names and circumstances still
crowding back upon her, as words written in lemon come out
upon exposure to a friendly warmth" (II, 78-79). Memory,
love, and kinship combined to make the meeting memorable.
The old farmhouse and the wholesome attributes of the
rural inhabitants give as much joy as the creations of art. The
qualities of holiness, calm, homeliness, and beneficence, generally associated with the imagination, were found in Hertfordshire. Art and reality fuse in "a sort of double singleness." Memory and imagination join to create art.

Thinking back on his many joyful memories, Elia closes
the essay:

When I forget all this, then may my country cousins forget me;
and Bridget no more remember, that in the days of weakling infancy I was her tender charge—as I have been her charge in
foolish manhood since—in those pretty pastoral walks long ago,
about Mackery End, in Hertfordshire.

(II, 79)

Shared memories will keep their experiences alive for
some time; the essay, however, is Elia's assurance that their
recollections will not be solely dependent on memory, which
is subject to decay, but given continuous existence in a work
of art.

During the course of the essay Elia glances several times
at decay and death. Features of Mackery End had changed;
both the pigeon house and the birds had disappeared. As
they decline, "old bachelor and maid," Elia and Bridget go
to their deaths, knowing that with their deaths the name
Elia ends. Elia, then, does have cause "to go out upon the
mountains with the rash king's offspring" (II, 75) to bewail
his celibacy. He refers to the almost complete extinction of
the Field line and to the death of Bridget, who is ten years
older than himself. "I wish," he writes, "that I could throw
into a heap the remainder of our joint existences, that we
might share them in equal division. But that is impossible"
(II, 77). But is it impossible, we ask ourselves. Does not Elia
assure himself and Bridget a sort of mutual existence in art,
which is a form of memory, just as mutual memories and the
ties of kinship proved to be stronger than the effects of forty
years' separation from Mackery End? Lamb is speaking in
the essay of three different bonds and relationships: the
bonds of friendship, the ties of kinship, and the union of
memory and the imagination. Memory, blood, and art are
types of continuity and immortality.

# IV

## TIME AND ETERNITY

*"The Superannuated Man"*

*"New Year's Eve"*

A STATE of peace, a sense of permanence, and a delight in the release from the rigors of life and from the demands of the conscience are generally associated with Lamb's conception of the imagination. His trust in the beauty of the imagination, however, does not prevent him from affirming the truths of life; he delights in reality and in the complexities of life.

After a visit to the Lake Country, Lamb wrote to Thomas Manning that although he was moved by the scenes in nature, he preferred the streets of London to Skiddaw:

Besides, after all, Fleet-Street and the Strand are better places to live in for good and all than among Skiddaw. Still, I turn back to those great places where I wandered about, participating in their greatness. After all, I could not *live* in Skiddaw. I could spend a year—two, three years—among them, but I must have a prospect of seeing Fleet-Street at the end of that time, or I should mope and pine away, I know.[1]

In another letter (28 November 1800) to Manning, Lamb refers to an invitation from Charles and Sophia Lloyd to spend some time with them at the Lakes:

For my part, with reference to my friends northward, I must confess that I am not romance-bit about *Nature*. The earth, and sea, and sky (when all is said) is but as a house to dwell in . . . Streets, streets, streets, markets, theatres, churches, Covent Gardens, shops sparkling with pretty faces of industrious milliners, neat sempstresses, ladies cheapening, gentlemen behind counters lying, authors in the street with spectacles, George Dyers (you may know them by their gait), lamps lit at night, pastry-cooks' and silver-smiths' shops, beautiful Quakers of Pentonville, noise of coaches, drowsy cry of mechanic watchmen at night, with bucks reeling home drunk; if you happen to wake at midnight, cries of Fire and Stop thief; inns of court, with their learned air, and halls, and butteries, just like Cambridge colleges; old bookstalls, Jeremy Taylors, Burtons on Melancholy, and Religio Medicis on every stall. These are thy pleasures, O London with-the-many-sins. O City abounding in whores, for these may Keswick and her giant brood go hang![2]

Lamb's spirited apostrophe to London reflects more than an exaggerated expression of his liking of the life of the city. For Lamb an embrace of London life ultimately meant a recognition and an acceptance of man as a fallen being. He preferred the town to the country, and civilization to innocence: it is because man made the city that Lamb

---

[1] *The Letters of Charles Lamb: To Which are Added Those of His Sister Mary*, ed. E. V. Lucas (London: J. H. Dent; Methuen, 1935), I, 316.

[2] *Letters*, I. 223-234.

enjoyed it so much. Man's fall from innocence brought experience, knowledge, civilization, and the sorrows and the joys unique to mankind, haunted by death, the final fruit of its sins. Although Lamb frequently voices a desire for an innocent, changeless, perfect state, he does not disdain

> All that man is,
> All mere complexities,
> The fury and the mire of human veins.[3]

Central to Lamb's understanding of man's nature is his awareness that to be human is to live in time. Freedom from time and attainment of maximum stability—immortality—are the death of man. As examples of Lamb's concern with time and eternity, life and death, I will discuss two essays, "The Superannuated Man" and "New Year's Eve."

In both essays we are invited to participate sympathetically, without judging, in the flow of experience in Elia's mind. Lamb's attention to the interior life of his creations in the essays can be compared to Browning's method in his dramatic monologues. His manner of presenting the thoughts of Elia in "The Superannuated Man" is much closer to Browning's method of revealing the mind of the duke of "My Last Duchess" than it is to the technique of the character, Elia's literary ancestor. In Lamb's essay and Browning's poem a similar method is used, whereby the narrator reveals much more about himself than he intends. Like Browning, Lamb involves us in a dramatic situation that is complicated by irony. And the irony is not dependent on an objective order of values outside the essay. Rather, because it is the result of the presentation of a particular human experience,

---

[3] W. B. Yeats, *The Collected Poems of W. B. Yeats* (New York: Macmillan, 1956), p. 243.

the irony is revelatory and dramatic: it is a means to explore the complexities of Elia's meditation and to undercut the literal meaning of his narrative.

A long periodic sentence introduces the subject of Elia's thoughts in "The Superannuated Man." He addresses us:

> If peradventure, Reader, it has been thy lot to waste the golden years of thy life—thy shining youth—in the irksome confinement of an office; to have thy prison days prolonged through middle age down to decrepitude and silver hairs, without hope of release or respite; to have lived to forget that there are such things as holidays, or to remember them but as the prerogatives of childhood; then, and then only, will you be able to appreciate my deliverance.[4]

Elia asks for our sympathy and understanding by pleading the bond between fellow sufferers. He announces the main interest of the sentence and of the essay—his release from the confinement and drudgery of the office—only after several qualifications in the dependent clause. The sentence is carefully developed to hold mention of Elia's deliverance in suspense for the length of one paragraph. The form of the sentence parallels the pattern of Elia's thought and introduces the basic form of the essay. Release of suspense in the final word of the last sentence of the paragraph reflects his feelings of joy and freedom at his unexpected retirement. Images and metaphors of imprisonment and of liberation inform the whole essay. Examples of freedom, such as holidays, vacations, and playtime, are contrasted with illustrations of confinement, such as cages, imprisonment, and servitude.

---

[4] *The Works of Charles and Mary Lamb,* ed. E. V. Lucas (London: Methuen, 1903-5), II, 193. Volume number and page numbers for subsequent quotations from the *Works* will be given in the text.

During the course of the essay, however, Elia's fondest
hopes of the advantages of retirement come true with a
vengeance. What he sees before his retirement as a state of
bondage appears to us at the end of the essay as responsible
for many of his pleasures in life. The essay is written after he
is retired, and the contrast between his expectations of the
freedom brought by leisure and the unexpected results of
the fulfillment of his dreams are suggested in the first paragraph. Elia is almost pleading too much, as if he were more
interested in convincing himself of the disadvantages of the
office than he is in gaining our understanding.

Elia spent thirty-six years as a clerk at his desk in Mincing Lane, coming there at age fourteen from the halcyon
days of school vacations and abundant playtime. He eventually overcame the melancholy period of transition and
"became content—doggedly contented, as wild animals in
cages" (II, 193). He still had Sundays to himself, but they
were, he says, particularly unsuitable for days of recreation.
He found the silence and emptiness gloomy, and missed the
ballad singers, the displays of tradesmen's wares, the cheerful sounds and bustle of crowded streets. The only sound
was the ringing of bells, and their constant pealing dis-
tressed him. He adds:

> The closed shops repel me. Prints, pictures, all the glittering and
> endless succession of knacks and gewgaws, and ostentatiously
> displayed wares of tradesmen, which make a week-day saunter
> through the less busy parts of the metropolis so delightful—are
> shut out. No book-stalls deliciously to idle over—No busy faces
> to recreate the idle man who contemplates them ever passing by
> —the very face of business a charm by contrast to his temporary
> relaxation from it.
>
> (II, 193-194)

As Elia describes what he misses on Sundays, he reveals the real source of his pleasures, the stir of life. The variety and contrast of street scenes give him pleasure and recreate his mind. Ironically a day of freedom and leisure does not bring him enjoyment. On Sundays there is a deadness in the air that vaguely foreshadows death. The only people he sees are those who, like himself, are out eagerly hunting pleasure, as if they thought that their free day should bring enjoyment. The very few people in the streets, "emancipated 'prentices and little tradesfolks, with here and there a servant maid" (II, 194), pursue their leisure, haunted by their hard duties of the week before and the knowledge that the hours of their holiday are fleeting. Although they have a free day, they do not have freedom; their expectations of the day are not met.

Besides Sundays Elia received a day of Easter and Christmas and a week's vacation in the summer. And yet, like his Sundays and like the free days of the servant maid, these holidays were "spent in restless pursuit of pleasure" (II, 194). He worked to enjoy himself and anxiously worried that the days were passing too quickly; his week vanished even before he had a taste of it. But, Elia adds, by anticipating the peace and quiet promised by his vacation, he made his thraldom at the office bearable the other fifty-one weeks of the year.

The rigors of his duties at the office, together with a haunting "sense of incapacity for business" (II, 194), affected Elia to such a degree that his health flagged; his worries even pursued him into his sleep. There appeared no hope of release from his servitude, since he was some years from retirement. "I was fifty years of age," Elia writes, "and no prospect of emancipation presented itself. I had grown to

my desk, as it were; and the wood had entered into my soul"
(II, 194). His fellow workers sometimes tried to raise Elia's
spirits, but his bad looks persisted and finally caught the attention of L., the junior partner in the firm, to whom Elia
admitted the cause of them.

Afraid that he had given the company grounds for dismissing him, Elia worried through each hour of the week
following their conversation, until one evening he was unex-
pectedly summoned to meet with the whole assembled firm.
Expecting to be fired, Elia was instead retired with a pen-
sion, two-thirds of his accustomed salary. The members of
the firm gathered about eight o'clock, and by ten minutes
after eight Elia was on his way home. The sudden fulfillment
of Elia's fondest hopes in ten minutes is contrasted with his
almost unimaginable expectations. These few minutes stand
out from the generally uneventful years, days, hours, and
minutes of his life before his retirement. Elia notes both the
day and the hour; it was the evening of the 12th of April,
from about eight o'clock to ten minutes after eight.

Elia's accounts of his existence as a clerk, of the events
leading to his retirement, and of the meeting with the whole
firm describe different experiences of time. Time is made
concrete through Elia's experience of it; time is subjective
and not something that exists independently of him. His desires, fears, and ambitions shape time, lengthening and tele-
scoping it. When he is on vacation, the days pass too
quickly. When he worries the week before his retirement,
the hours are tediously long. Fifty-one weeks of the year go
by uneventfully, yet ten minutes of his life are filled with
momentous consequences. His servitude at the office and
the entanglement of life's duties, although they are the cause
for legitimate complaints, are the reason that Elia feels time.

And, as we soon realize, an awareness of time is essential to his human condition.

Having now presented the conditions of his life previous to his retirement, Elia continues the pattern established in the opening paragraph of the essay and describes his state of deliverance. By using his own calculations to determine time —"For *that* is the only true Time, which a man can properly call his own, that which he has all to himself" (II, 196)—Elia computes that his next ten years will equal his preceding thirty. Given an apparent eternity of time, "for it is a sort of Eternity for a man to have his Time all to himself" (II, 195), with the means to enjoy it, Elia is at first overwhelmed by the enormity of his good fortune. Like the prisoner set free after many years' confinement, Elia can only appreciate his freedom mentally: it is several days before he can "taste it sincerely" (II, 195). In fact he is disappointed at first. Having looked forward to these days so long, he pretends to be happy, although he is not, because he feels that he should be. He was a stranger in eternity, who was free to do everything but did little.

Elia realizes somewhat that a sudden release from the pressing concerns of daily life is not altogether desirable, and he would "caution persons grown old in active business, not lightly, nor without weighing their own resources, to forego their customary employment all at once, for there may be danger in it" (II, 195-196). Apparently in a position to be giving advice, Elia does not realize just how mixed a blessing his liberation is. The irony of his situation becomes apparent to us, as he complacently details the blessedness of his condition. From the tediousness of forced activity he goes to what appears the boredom of inactivity:

I am in no hurry. Having all holidays, I am as though I had none. If Time hung heavy upon me, I could walk it away; but I do *not* walk all day long, as I used to do in those old transient holidays, thirty miles a day, to make the most of them. If Time were troublesome, I could read it away, but I do *not* read in that violent measure, with which having no Time my own but candle-light Time, I used to weary out my head and eyesight in by-gone winters. I walk, read or scribble (as now) just when the fit seizes me. I no longer hunt after pleasure; I let it come to me.

(II, 196)

Before his superannuation, because time was precious, it was felt and fully used. In his new state time is troublesome and, at times, hangs heavy upon him. Elia really has no holidays, but not quite in the sense he thinks. Holidays were once distinct days, because they were looked forward to and regretted when over; now they no longer have any meaning, since all his days are holidays, and therefore alike. His holidays were not always enjoyable, but because they were transient, they were at least felt as days different from other days.

Elia does not realize it, but his days were different because they were felt as tedious, as precious, or as fleeting. Rich in time and money, he is a poorer man; retirement is really an impoverishment of his existence, not a blessing. His italicized "nots" in the passage quoted above—Elia considers it a source of pride that he is not doing things—are an ironic comment on his condition. His longing anticipations of rest and quiet are being met with an ironic vengeance.

In his new state of timelessness, Elia is dissociated from any web of shared experiences. Removed from association with his friends at the Counting House, Elia found that the clerks with whom he had "for so many years, and for so many hours in each day of the year, been closely associated—being

suddenly removed from them—they seemed as dead to me"
(II, 196). Elia emphasizes the length of time spent with his
fellow clerks, as if he regrets that he no longer shares days,
and hours, and experiences with them. He returns to the
familiar surroundings of the counting house for several visits
with the friends who had smoothed some of his labors. They
momentarily revive some pleasant memories, and Elia even
has some misgivings about his harsh judgment of his years at
the firm, an indulgence he could permit himself, since he no
longer worked there. He wonders: "Had it been so rugged
then after all? or was I a coward simply?" (II, 197). Elia is
without things to do and without someone with whom to
share his eternity of time; he is in fact the man who is dead.
In an apostrophe he bids farewell to his old cronies, to the
Merchant House, and to the volumes containing his accounts.
His leave-taking suggests that he has broken all ties with his
past and that he can turn to the rest of his days with complete equanimity.

The last part of the essay is ostensibly written two weeks
after Elia's first communication. At that time he was nearing
a state of tranquillity but had not reached it. At first, after
his retirement, like "a poor Carthusian, from strict cellular
discipline suddenly by some revolution returned upon the
world" (II, 197), Elia missed his old chains, as if they had
been some necessary part of his apparel. His very chains and
he grew friends. Elia, however, is unlike both the prisoner of
the Bastille, mentioned earlier in the essay, and the Carthusian monk, because they were released from confinement
into the world, whereas Elia withdrew from the world into
a state similar to death.

There is a lifelessness now associated with Elia's activities. He writes: "I find myself at eleven o'clock in the day in

Bond-street, and it seems to me that I have been sauntering there at that very hour for years past. I digress into Soho, to explore a book-stall. Methinks I have been thirty years a collector. There is nothing strange nor new in it" (II, 197). He wistfully wonders what clerk walks down Mincing Lane now. Streets, because they are no longer associated with his feelings, are indistinct. All sense of time is lost. Years, seasons, months, days, and hours—are all indistinct. Each day used to be felt in reference to other days:

> I had my Wednesday feelings, my Saturday nights' sensations. The genius of each day was upon me distinctly during the whole of it, affecting my appetite, spirits, &c. The phantom of the next day, with the dreary five to follow, sate as a load upon my poor Sabbath recreations. What charm has washed that Ethiop white? What is gone of Black Monday? All days are the same. Sunday itself—that unfortunate failure of a holyday as it too often proved, what with my sense of its fugitiveness, and over-care to get the greatest quantity of pleasure out of it—is melted down into a week day.
>
> (II, 198)

Elia now takes Lucretian pleasure in disinterestedly watching drudges labor on. Congratulating himself that he no longer has to work and convinced that man "is out of his element as long as he is operative," Elia concludes that he is "altogether for the life contemplative" (II, 198). But it is because Elia is no longer operative that he is no longer human. He has melted down from a vital being to a personification. He brags: "I am no longer . . . clerk to the Firm of &c. I am Retired Leisure. I am to be met with in trim gardens. I am already come to be known by my vacant face and careless gesture, perambulating at no fixed pace, nor with any settled purpose. I walk about; not to and from" (II, 198). Elia's new state is certainly an uneventful ending to high hopes and a pale conclusion to eager anticipations of the advantages of leisure. The liberation from that which Elia most dislikes, that is, the cares of life and the fugitiveness of time, have ironically deprived him of the pleasures and pains of a human being. He finally loses all sense of life. The human condition, Lamb understands, is defined by our enslavement to time.

Besides the literal and ironic levels of interest in the essay, there is a third level of meaning. All feelings and desires attributed to Elia are psychologically accurate and realistically presented. And yet, without distorting or violating the psychological facts, Lamb's development of Elia's thoughts and feelings about his imprisonment at the office and his subsequent deliverance suggests an analogue for the differences between the states of life and death. Eschatological matters are rarely confronted in the essays; rather, death is viewed obliquely through man's mundane experiences. Elia's confinement at the office represents his condition as a human being; his retirement prefigures his life after death.

I have already noted that metaphors of imprisonment and release occur frequently in the essay. The Platonic tradition in Western civilization regarded life as a fall from eternity into the human condition; death was a blessed state of release from the tangled affairs of the world. Timelessness and inactivity were commonly used to characterize man's state after deliverance from a life of "task work" (II, 199). Once Lamb's intentions are gathered, a few phrases throughout the essay keep the analogy before our mind. Elia's walks down old Mincing Lane were a "daily pilgrimage" (II, 198). His release from the imprisonment of the office, or the world, is as sudden as an unexpected death. "It was no hyperbole," he writes, "when I ventured to compare the change in my condition to a passing into another world. Time stands still in a manner to me" (II, 198).

Elia's retirement is followed by a sense of unreality: he had the feeling that he was separated from his former existence by an irreversible tract of time. Drudges were "left behind in the world, carking and caring" (II, 198), and former friends at the Counting House, "cobrethren of the quill," he "had left below in the state militant" (II, 198). Elia, we presume, is in heaven with the members of the state triumphant. He suggests as much at the conclusion of the essay, where he writes: "*Opus operatum est.* I have worked task work, and have the rest of the day to myself" (II, 199). Elia is trying to express his feelings upon his retirement: Lamb suggests that the other world is the state of death. Elia's rewards at retirement are tenfold: "From a poor man, poor in Time, I was suddenly lifted up into a vast revenue" (II, 195).

Lamb sympathetically describes Elia's very human desires for freedom from a burdened life of disappointments and unfulfilled desires, but he also reveals how these desires, when fulfilled, are themselves unsatisfactory. And Lamb appears unwilling to give up his humanity for the life of a spirit. He implies that he would rather enjoy the comforts and disappointments of this world than experience the ethereal rewards of a disembodied soul, that he would rather enjoy the green earth than intuit knowledge like an angel.

Release from the cares of existence into a state of stasis is a frequently expressed theme in the poetry of his contemporaries. I wonder if Lamb is not measuring this desire. Far from wanting to escape life, Lamb, in the essays, embraces life, both its good and its ill fortunes. He expresses his feelings about earthly comforts in a letter to Robert Lloyd (13 November 1798):

> the Bees are wiser in their generation than the race of sonnet writers and complainers, Bowle's and Charlotte Smiths, and all that tribe, who can see no joys but what are past, and fill people's heads with notions of the unsatisfying nature of Earthly comforts. I assure you I find this world a very pretty place.[5]

The joys that are past and the comforts of this world are the subject of Lamb's essay "New Year's Eve."

In "New Year's Eve" Elia's mind moves from sober reflections on the past to an eager embrace of the future. The change in his mind is not merely an exercise in contrasting views of New Year's Eve; rather, the shift is rooted in Elia's experiences and his meditations on them. The passing of an Old Year moves Elia to the thought that he is one year nearer death, as are all men. The birth of a New Year "is the nativity of our common Adam" (II, 27), since we all share in our first father's death.

Elia is especially moved on New Year's Eve by the sound of bells, tolling the death knell of the Old Year. He subjectively humanizes the abstraction time. At the sound of bells he looks back on the past year from the perspective of what he has suffered, performed, or neglected; the Old Year takes on a "personal colour" (II, 27) for him. Unlike his companions, who "affected rather to manifest an exhilaration at the birth of the coming year, than any very tender regrets for the decease of its predecessor" (II, 27), Elia mourns the Old Year, as if time had become an old and dear companion. He is none of those who "welcome the coming,

---

[5] *Letters*, I, 138.

speed the parting guest."[6] In fact Elia claims that regret for the past is a habit with him.

Naturally shy of novelties, he prefers to dwell on the experiences and disappointments of the past. Elia is most comfortable with what he is most familiar. His past experiences are immutable and make no demands on him, so that he can view them objectively. None of those who look to new books, new faces, and new years with anticipation, Elia has almost given up hope, and is

> sanguine only in the prospects of other (former) years. I plunge into foregone visions and conclusions. I encounter pell-mell with past disappointments. I am armour-proof against old discouragements. I forgive, or overcome in fancy, old adversaries. I play over again *for love,* as the gamesters phrase it, games, for which I once paid so dear. I would scarce now have any of those untoward accidents and events of my life reversed. I would not more alter them than the incidents of some well-contrived novel.
> (II, 28)

The materials of his retrospection are not singularly happy, and yet Elia would be unwilling to change any part of his past. Even the gravest disappointments of his life, his thwarted love for Alice W---n and the loss of a family legacy to old Dorell, he could not bear to lose. Elia feels that it is better to have suffered these disappointments than not to have had these experiences at all. So Elia's unwillingness to look with eagerness to the future is not simply a desire to escape from life into the past, because he does not regret even the painful experiences of his life.

Elia admits that his habit of looking back on his early days is a weakness, and asks whether he advances a paradox when he says, "that, skipping over the intervention of forty

---

[6] Quoted by Lamb from Pope's *Odyssey,* XV, 84, and "Second Satire of Horace," Book II, 160.

years, a man may have leave to love *himself*, without the imputation of self-love?" (II, 28). The contrast between what he is as an adult and what he was as a child appears so great to Elia that he feels there is no sense of continuity between the two. Now he is vain, light, and guilty of shortcomings too horrible to spell out plainly. He even invites us to join him in a chorus of depreciation. Elia exaggerates his shortcomings to make the contrast with the child more forceful; he can love himself without the charge of egotism because the child seems to have no relationship whatsoever to the adult Elia. And so Elia can love the child as if he were another person. Elia would subscribe to any charge made against him, but he would exempt from his dislike the child Elia, that " 'other me' " (II, 28), so unlike Elia, it is as if it had been born of some other house and not of his parents.

The child does not appear to be the father of the man Elia. Elia could weep tender tears for that dear, honest child: "how courageous (for a weakling) it was—how religious, how imaginative, how hopeful! From what have I not fallen, if the child I remember was indeed myself,—and not some dissembling guardian, presenting a false identity, to give the rule to my unpractised steps, and regulate the tone of my moral being!" (II, 28). In spite of the high regard for the child, Elia's childhood memories, like the recollections of his more immediate past, are not pleasant. They are of a small-pox patient at five and of the child's "poor fevered head upon the sick pillow at Christ's" (II, 28). That Elia, then, should indulge in such retrospection may be, as he suggests, "the symptom of some sickly idiosyncrasy. Or is it owing to another cause; simply, that being without wife or family, I have not learned to project myself enough out of myself; and having no offspring of my own to dally with, I turn back upon

memory, and adopt my own early idea, as my heir and fa-
vourite?" (II, 28-29). Elia's latter explanation is most plausible,
when we consider the materials of his recollections. Because
he did not marry an Alice W---n, he now faces death without
the consolation afforded an old man by his children. Unlike
the child at Christ's and the smallpox patient, Elia's awareness of death is felt.

Even when he was a child, the ringing of bells started a
pensive train of thought in Elia on New Year's Eve; yet his
knowledge of mortality was cerebral and not proved upon
his pulses. The child knows but he does not feel his immortality as a chilling fact of his existence. Elia's child shares
with Wordsworth's child in the "Intimations Ode" "an indis-
position to bend to the law of death, as applying to our [his]
own particular case."[7] He then scarce conceived what death
meant, or thought of it as a reckoning that concerned him.
In fact, Elia writes:

> Not childhood alone, but the young man till thirty, never feels
> practically that he is mortal. He knows it indeed, and, if need
> were, he could preach a homily on the fragility of life; but he
> brings it not home to himself, any more than in a hot June we can
> appropriate to our imagination the freezing days of December.
> But now, now shall I confess a truth?—I feel these audits but too
> powerfully.
>
> (II, 29)

As Elia reluctantly thinks on his own death, he dis-
misses traditional consolations. That all men must die, that
death is the leveler, or that it promises rest after earthly trials

---

[7] From a statement by William Wordsworth, in a letter to Cath-
erine Clarkson, December 1814, with reference to the "Intimations
Ode," *The Letters of William and Dorothy Wordsworth: The Middle
Years*, ed. Ernest de Selincourt (Oxford: Clarendon Press, 1937), II,
619.

do not "sweeten the unpalatable draught of mortality" (II, 29). In a passage similar to Wordsworth's lines,

> Not in Utopia,—subterranean fields,—
> Or some secreted island, Heaven knows where!
> But in the very world, which is the world
> Of all of us,—the place where, in the end,
> We find our happiness, or not at all![8]

Elia, unwilling to leave behind the simple pleasures of a day, speaks of his love for

> this green earth; the face of town and country; the unspeakable rural solitudes, and the sweet security of streets. I would set up my tabernacle here. I am content to stand still at the age to which I am arrived; I, and my friends: to be no younger, no richer, no handsomer. I do not want to be weaned by age; or drop, like mellow fruit, as they say, into the grave.
>
> (II, 29)

Elia's quest for permanence is a desire for a humanized eternity, for a heaven on earth. He would frustrate the cycle of birth, life, and death, and stop life in a pulsing moment of the present. His wish to stand still in the present and his habit of returning to the past have similar results. In both the past and in a static present he would be free from the uncertainties of existence, its accidents and disappointments, and finally from mortality. Yet to live in the past or in a still present would be a certain kind of death, similar to the state of the frozen figures on Keats's urn. Elia's life is meaningful only because it is haunted by mortality.

A dramatic shift has occurred in the essay, which began with sober thoughts on death and wistful glances at Elia's lost childhood. As Elia confesses to us his fear of death, he

---

[8] *The Prelude,* ed. Ernest de Selincourt (Oxford: Clarendon Press, 1926), XI, 142-144.

expresses a desire to hoard the minutes of his remaining years. His meditations have shifted from the past to the present and will move to an open embrace of the future. Elia would stay time to preserve his pleasures, not yet realizing that the reason these experiences are sweet is that they occur in time and are fleeting. An acceptance of life is a voyage to death. And yet, for Elia, unable even to accept any move from his familiar lodgings, the thought of a new state is beyond his comprehension. He tries to imagine a bodiless existence, where all the delights of human life would be left behind. Are they to be snuffed out and exchanged for ghostly abstractions? He asks:

> Sun, and sky, and breeze, and solitary walks, and summer holidays, and the greenness of fields, and the delicious juices of meats and fishes, and society, and the cheerful glass, and candle-light, and fire-side conversations, and innocent vanities, and jests, and *irony itself*—do these things go out with life?
>
> (II, 29)

As Elia wonders about the loss of pleasures in a state after death, he is lamenting the loss of distinctly human pleasures. He is in effect now generating the reasons for a turn to the future. His pleasures are human and dependent on his acceptance of the human condition, which is precarious and finite. But as long as he begrudges the future welcome, he denies himself time, which creates his humanity and his pleasures. Thoughts on death and the subsequent loss of human pleasures, however, gradually bring Elia closer to an acceptance of the future.

That he now turns to the seasons to express his thoughts on life and death reveals that he is closer than before to accepting the cycle of existence. He is most haunted by death in winter, a season devoid of life. In autumn the sense of the fullness of life is so intense that "death is almost problematic" (II, 30). Then a man almost convinces himself, buoyed confidently by life burgeoning around him, that he will not die. Fall frosts, however, bring thoughts of death, an odious deprivation, which Elia now curses. His protests against death bring him to an acceptance of the New Year, because it brings with it time and human pleasures. To the dead man who lectures him from his tombstone that he must shortly die, Elia says:

> Not so shortly, friend, perhaps, as thou imaginest. In the meantime I am alive. I move about. I am worth twenty of thee. Know thy betters! Thy New Years' Days are past. I survive, a jolly candidate for 1821. Another cup of wine—and while that turn-coat bell, that just now mournfully chanted the obsequies of 1820 departed, with changed notes lustily rings in a successor, let us attune to its peal the song made on a like occasion, by hearty, cheerful Mr. Cotton.
>
> (II, 31)

The essay has moved full circle from meditations on the past to an acceptance of the future. The shift in Elia's mind is signaled by the mention of bells. At the beginning of the essay the bell "mournfully chanted the obsequies of 1820 departed;" now, "with changed notes lustily rings in a successor" (II, 31). The same object that peals out the Old Year rings in the New and, ironically, Elia has become one of those who "welcome the coming, speed the parting guest." The method of the essay is similar to the movement of Coleridge's poem "Frost at Midnight." Like the objects in Coleridge's poem, the bells provide a frame for the essay and point up the dramatic movement of Elia's mind.

Elia embraces the New Year because it defies death. He has found not an antidote to death but rather an affirmation

of the human condition—even in its precariousness. Even intense disappointments would be preferable to a bodiless
existence and so he warmly embraces the legacy of the future. Only by confronting death does Elia gain his life; by
accepting time, he defeats it and accepts his humanity. There
is a Keatsian acceptance of the human, and of time that both
ravages and creates. Death, because it stalks every man, is
inextricably bound up with the human predicament. It
ironically becomes man's ally. As Elia reflects on his past, we
realize that if Elia were to deny the future, he would deny
time and his humanity. Time renews itself each New Year's,
as does Elia.

Cotton's poem, "The New Year," quoted by Elia, repeats
the pattern of the essay. Like Elia, the speaker of the poem
takes a melancholy glimpse at the parting of the Old Year
and looks anxiously into the future; at the end of the poem
he looks forward, like the "turn-coat bell," to the future with
eagerness, because it brings the pleasures that the Old Year
gave. Cotton's poem cleanses Elia of all fear of death. Lamb
hopes that the product of his imagination will liberate us
from the fear of death and lead us to accept our paradoxical
state. To accept time is to accept death. Yet time's passing
brings our unique sorrows and joys. We are human because
we die.

The final irony is that the child Elia is in fact the father
of the regenerated Elia. At the end of the essay Elia has in
common with the child hope, imagination, and trust in life.
Meditation on his experience has regenerated him, because
as he reviews his past he clings to all his experiences. Elia
shares with the child Elia at Christ's the disinclination to die.
The fevered child could die; but he only knows and does not
feel death. As Elia comes to realize the fear of death, he still

shares with the child an unwillingness to die. There is a continuity of experience. Recollections themselves renew Elia. At first they only provide occasion for a painful contrast with his present state of existence, but they also provide the material for the imagination to renew itself, as it turns from a longing for the past to the gleeful greeting of the future. Acceptance of the future accompanies a sense of personal renewal and integration. The bells that ring out the Old Year and toll in the New also moved Elia when he was a child. The persistence of the object in Elia's thoughts reflects the continuity between the child and Elia. Whereas Wordsworth uses images from nature to develop his ode, Elia uses the pattern of a human experience. The workings of the human mind, not nature, provide Lamb with a vehicle for his conceptions.

# V

## TO TEACH AND TO DELIGHT

*"Old China"*

O NE of Wordsworth's favorites among the last essays attributed to Elia, "Old China" evidently was also highly regarded by Lamb. With the exception of the collection of shorter pieces titled "Popular Fallacies," he placed the essay, first published in 1823, at the end of the collection of the essays published in 1833. It is the culmination of *The Essays of Elia* and exemplifies the elements of Lamb's art.

We have seen that Lamb frequently examines differences between art and reality in many of the essays. In "Old China" he demonstrates his balanced genius at the height of its powers, which holds as valid both the practical world of reality and the world of the imagination. The essay exhibits his belief that the imagination and the understanding are not antagonistic faculties. A domestic setting, an unassuming object, and a frame—all used in this essay—also characterize the method of Lamb's art in a number of the essays. References to a teacup, which is the object of Elia's thoughts, open and close the essay.

That Lamb uses a form similar to that of other essays of Elia, and that he returns to themes already familiar to us are fitting reasons to end my study of the essays with a discussion of "Old China."

Elia begins the essay by admitting to "an almost feminine partiality for old china" (II, 247). When he goes to see a great house, he asks to see the china closet before the picture gallery. His confession makes him appear a little vulnerable and something of an old maid, but his manner, frank and conversational, and his fondness for china are our way into the essay. By giving the impression that he has nothing to hide, Elia gains our confidence; since we feel that he has no designs on us, we relax, unaware that we are preparing ourselves to participate sympathetically in his meditation. Ostensibly an unpromising subject for the activity of the imagination, a china teacup is perfectly suited to the form and the themes of the essay: it is a fragile object that combines the utilitarian and the aesthetic. Elia refers to both aspects of china—its uses as tableware and as an object of enjoyment—when he mentions that he and Bridget are using a recently purchased set of china for the first time, and that he finds "trifles of this sort" (II, 248) pleasing to the eye. The dual nature of the teacup reflects Lamb's conceptions of imagination and understanding as complementary modes of experience. The teacup, then, provides both the matter for Elia's thought and the means to present an ordered movement of consciousness.

As Elia's attention focuses on a china teacup, the language shifts from a prose of statement to a prose of images and meditation. The movement of his mind during the meditation, increasingly identifying itself with the figures on the teacup, is similar to the method used by Keats in the "Ode on a Grecian Urn."[1] When Elia was a child, he was not disturbed by the world that he saw on a china teacup. Whereas he believes that the child could imaginatively observe the lawless world there, Elia suggests, in a parenthetical question, that there is some uncertainty in his mind about his adult reaction to the indistinct world on a teacup:

> I had no repugnance then—why should I now have?—to those little, lawless, azure—tinctured grotesques, that under the notion of men and women, float about, uncircumscribed by any element, in that world before perspective—a china tea-cup.
> I like to see my old friends—whom distance cannot diminish—figuring up in the air (so they appear to our optics), yet on *terra firma* still—for so we must in courtesy interpret that speck of deeper blue, which the decorous artist, to prevent absurdity, has made to spring up beneath their sandals.
>
> (II, 248)

Two centers of consciousness, the understanding and the imagination, are present throughout the several paragraphs describing Elia's thoughts about a piece of china. "Daylight understanding" (II, 141) and our senses, such as the eye ("our optics"), are accustomed to the laws of logic and perspective, but these laws do not hold true on the teacup, where Elia sees grotesques floating about in an undefined space. These figures correspond to the chaotic materials of the imagination at the start of its activity.

---

[1] I am indebted to Richard Haven's "The Romantic Art of Charles Lamb," *ELH*, 30 (1963), 137-146, for some of my observations in this chapter.

Space is uncircumscribed on the teacup, yet the men and women on it are not completely unlocalized, since the artist had painted a hint of blue beneath them. The speck of color and the indistinct figures are the plastic materials, the *materia prima,* demanded by the shaping imagination. To the eye the men and women seem "figuring in the air," but to the eye of the imagination they are on solid ground. As the meditation continues and the imagination exercises its powers, the scene and the figures become increasingly more detailed. When Elia describes a Mandarin, his imagination has fully warmed to its task:

> Here is a young and courtly Mandarin, handing tea to a lady from a salver—two miles off. See how distance seems to set off respect?! And here the same lady, or another—for likeness is identity on tea-cups—is stepping into a little fairy boat, moored on the hither side of this calm garden river, with a dainty mincing foot, which in a right angle of incidence (as angles go in our world) must infallibly land her in the midst of a flowery mead—a furlong off on the other side of the same strange stream!
>
> (II, 248)

"Here" announces a shift in point of view. The "I" of Elia has given way to the objective point of view of a pictorial sketch. Subject and object meet in the liberating energies of the imagination, so that the mind and the materials of the observable world create a new reality. Not only are the characteristics of a Mandarin described, but the salver that he offers to the lady is also noted. What was first uncircumscribed space and later specks of blue is now a boat on a river and a flowery mead. Although the world on the teacup now appears more like the real world than it did earlier, the laws of space are still transcended by the imagination. However distinct the figures are, their actions are still lawless, "as

angles go in our world." Distance is seen not from the viewpoint of the senses but as a symbol to the imagination of respect for the lady. The actions of the lady who is stepping
into a fairy boat seem strange and ludicrous to the understanding and the senses but not to a child's mind or to a
poetic talent. Because the imagination is limited by reality
but not to it, perspective and actions on the teacup conform
to the world of the imagination, not to laws of Euclidean
geometry.

By the end of Elia's monologue the animating powers
of the mind have added "horses, trees, pagodas, dancing the
hays," and "a cow and rabbit couchant, and coextensive—so
objects show, seen through the lucid atmosphere of fine
Cathay" (II, 248). The clarity of the atmosphere parallels
the lucidity of the imagination. There is order in the creations
of the imagination, but it is not the order that would be given
by the understanding, which categorizes, differentiates, and
judges; rather, it is a harmonious world, where animals,
trees, and buildings join in a joyful, old English dance—long
a symbol of order and harmony.

As Elia passes from his meditation on the teacup to a
conversation that he had with Bridget the evening before,
during their tea, he returns, for the moment, to the use of
"I," indicating that his mind and the teacup are no longer
fused in a creative relationship. "I was pointing out to my
cousin last evening," he writes, "over our Hyson (which we
are old fashioned enough to drink unmixed still of an after-
noon) some of these *speciosa miracula* upon a set of extra-
ordinary old blue china (a recent purchase) which we were
now for the first time using" (II, 248). Elia's apparently
trivial asides contribute to the illusion of reality and immediacy, and keep the essay rooted in the materials of observa-

tion. "The common growth of mother-earth"[2] suffices Lamb
for his art: his mind feeds on life's daily fare. Like the young
Mandarin and his lady, the Elias are at tea, but unlike them,
Bridget and Elia do not participate in the never-changing
world of art. The adjectives "old fashioned" and "recent" remind us that we are back in a world subject to time.

As he had earlier with the figures on the teacup, Elia
identifies himself with Bridget, who now becomes the center
of consciousness in the essay. During Elia's meditation on
the teacup, art was limited by the understanding; reality is
now transformed by the imagination into the materials of
art. Reminiscence, nostalgia, and reality now become the
material for meditation. Her mind charged by pleasant recollections, Bridget recounts their happier days, when their
pleasures lay in speculation, anticipation, and weighing *"for
and against"* (II, 249). She attributes their pleasures, when
they purchased a folio or a print, to their circumstances at
the time, particularly to their poverty. Then a purchase was
the occasion for discussion and careful planning; now it can
be made at will.

She misses the good old days when they were not as
rich as now, and when they were happier coveting "a cheap
luxury" (II, 248). If one estimated only the amount of money
spent, the purchase was inexpensive; but if one considered
the sacrifice that the Elias made to buy the object out of their
meager means, or that the purchase of a Beaumont and
Fletcher folio meant foregoing a badly needed new suit, then
the purchase was a luxury. Furthermore, their desires, their

---

[2] William Wordsworth, *The Poetical Works of William Wordsworth*, ed. E. de Selincourt and Helen Darbisshire, 2nd ed. (Oxford:
Clarendon Press, 1953), II, 336.

feelings, and their hopes increased the value of an object, and they felt the money that they paid for it.

In subsequent recollections Bridget's argument is the same: a difficulty overcome or a sacrifice made heightened their pleasure. The haze of memory hallows their simple activities and common delights. They relished their outings, because they were undertaken in a spirit of adventure, or because they were precarious and evanescent. Infrequent attendance at the theater, for example, increased their pleasure when they did go, and "a little difficulty overcome [in getting to their places] heightened the snug seat, and the play, afterwards!" (II, 250). Now there is an inevitability and mechanical quality about their purchases and delights. Bridget complains: "Now you can only pay our money, and walk in. You cannot see, you say, in the galleries now. I am sure we saw, and heard too, well enough then—but sight, and all, I think, is gone with our poverty" (II, 250). Bridget, however, confuses the loss of all these youthful pleasures with the loss of their poverty. Hardships and difficulties contributed to their relationship and pleasures when they were young, but the resilient spirit of youth has passed away.

Elia admits the truth of her observation, that they were happier when they were poorer, but he reminds her: "we were also younger, my cousin" (II, 251). He regrets but accepts the loss of their youth, and returns to a pleasure that has been persistent, that of enjoying old china. It is while he is tenderly recollecting their delicious enjoyments at the theater that he returns to the china teacup: "And now do just look at that merry little Chinese waiter holding an umbrella, big enough for a bed-tester, over the head of that pretty insipid half-Madona-ish chit of a lady in that very blue summer-house" (II, 252). Elia indirectly reminds Bridget that

the imagination provides a constant source of pleasure beyond the reach of time, because it is not dependent on any
circumstances, such as youth or poverty.

For the imagination there is no need for a sense of
shame or an awareness of difficulties overcome to heighten
its enjoyments, although Elia's strong feelings, generated by
memories of the past, strengthen the intense experience of
his imagination. He returns to an incongruous world of a
very blue summerhouse and an umbrella large enough for
a bed-tester. Incongruity is not an affront to the imagination
but actually a relief from the burdens of time. Like the actions of the figures described earlier, the action of the Chinese waiter has neither a beginning nor an end. "Waiting" describes an action in progress and suggests that his action will
never end. The activities of the waiter, the mandarin, and the
lady stepping into a boat share in the permanence of art.
Their actions are inconsequential and impractical, and present a vision of perpetual enjoyment.

Bridget's recollections, however, describe a world very
much circumscribed and lawful, where cause and effect operate. It is a world of beginning and end, in contrast to the
continuous world of the circular china cup, where the laws of
space and time are not operative. Time, which is allied to
the Elias' youthful pleasures, is eventually also their enemy.
It lends a piquancy to their delights, but it eventually brings
with it the dissolution of them. And so follows the quest for
permanence in art. The essay's apparent insignificance belies
its permanent value: it is also, like the teacup, a world to be
entered. Elia gives life to the figures on the teacup, and Lamb
asks that we give eternal life to Bridget and Elia.

As Elia passes from his review of the memories recol-
lected by Bridget to mention old china again, the two parts

of the essay fuse. The immediate shift to the teacup, without any break such as a new paragraph, reflects Elia's ability to slip easily from one world of experience to another, whether it be of the memory, the understanding, or the imagination. Lamb forges a vision that encompasses both art and reality: in the best of his essays he demonstrates a unified sensibility that accepts the knowledge of the understanding and the truths of the imagination. His is an art of "so many diverse yet co-operating materials" (I, 77). The domestic setting, numerous asides, the sense of immediacy, Bridget's recollections, references to London life, its shops and booksellers contribute to the illusion of reality. The Latin quotation from Horace, Elia's meditation on old china, and his references to the theater, Izaak Walton, a Leonardo print, or a Beaumont and Fletcher folio are materials drawn from the world of art.

In the "Sanity of True Genius" Elia argues that neither a literal imitation of life nor the most extravagant creation of a frenzied mind guarantees an artist that his fiction will be successful art. Lamb avoided in his art both the tapestried world of gorgeous palaces (the prose of pure escape) and the drab world of everyday reality. His art reflects a sort of romantic realism. He maintains an illusion of reality even while he creates his most delicate artifacts, and he gives a sense of beauty even to the most unpromising subjects. Elia also argues in the same essay that "the greatness of wit, by which the poetic talent is here chiefly to be understood, manifests itself in the admirable balance of all the faculties" (II, 187). His judgment of genius is applicable to the best of Lamb's essays. Like a china teacup, his art is both useful and entertaining, thereby fulfilling Horace's requirement of art, that it be *dulce et utile*. Lamb's is not an "unpremeditated art"[3] but the creation of a poetic talent that manifests itself in a balance of all its faculties, and that wants to teach and to delight.

---

[3] Percy Bysshe Shelley, *Complete Works* (Julian ed.), ed. Roger Ingpen and W. E. Peck (New York: Scribners, 1926-30), III, 302.

# CONCLUSION

BECAUSE there are similarities of character between Elia and Charles Lamb, and between Lamb's essays and his letters and conversations, it is easy to assume that Elia is merely a thin disguise for Lamb. The failure to distinguish between Elia and his creator, however, has perhaps most hindered intelligent readings of the essays. Many readers of Lamb, even those who voice their respect for the essays of Elia, have fallen victim to Lamb's art. Beneath his pretense of simplicity, taken by some as simple-mindedness, there is a very complex and careful artist.

By pretending unimportance Lamb hoped to lull the reader's moral and critical faculties to sleep, so that he would suspend his sense of disapprobation and let his imagination exercise its function. Since Lamb said very little about his ambitions and intentions as an artist—he did not give us any fully developed expressions of his theory of art as did Wordsworth, Coleridge, or Shelley—we have to look to his practice in the *Essays of Elia* for his conceptions of art, imagination, and the distinctive qualities of an aesthetic experience. Lamb's ideas are not insisted upon or even explicit in the essays; rather, they form an integral part of his work.

Lamb tried to shape an aesthetic response to the essays by the character of Elia, his choice of the unpretentious essay form, and his selection of humble subjects and trivial objects for the matter of his essays. These elements of his art create the illusion that the essays are outside the practical world of experience and reality. Lamb realized that art is not a mirroring of the real world but an illusion that invites a spirit of imaginative contemplation. But this desire to have his essays treated as art does not mean that Lamb shunned reality or the experience of the understanding.

It is significant that man, architecture, and artifacts, not nature, provide Lamb with his most frequently used images and symbols. Man's shaping presence is at the center of Lamb's consciousness. Although the desire for calm and permanence is frequently expressed in his work, Lamb embraces time and change, since he realizes that an awareness of time is essential to the human condition. As a result of his sins, man must die, but his acceptance of time gives him his humanity, art, and civilization.

While the romantic poets were experimenting with a poetry of sincerity, Lamb was very quietly creating a prose of spontaneity and reflective immediacy by adapting the essay form to the mediative mood. In some essays he points ahead to the method of Robert Browning in the dramatic monologues in his use of the movement of consciousness of the narrator as a vehicle for his themes, so that the essays of Elia are revelatory and dramatic not discursive, argumentative, or informative. From Wordsworth and Coleridge he probably learned the method of using narrative to express and embody his thoughts. Lamb frequently uses setting and objects in it to give the essays their thematic and artistic unity: observable reality and the mind join to create a new reality.

The objects in Elia's essays are never merely occasions for an imaginative flight which spirals its way from the object to some transcendent reality; rather, they provide the matter for meditation and give the essay coherence. The genius of Lamb's imagination is that he can transform the mundane details of a daily existence into significant art without destroying their reality. Many readers of the essays regard his liking for unassuming objects as an expression of his interest in trivia. Lamb, however, together with the other romantics, contributed to the creation of an aesthetic climate so that the selection of such objects as cups and saucers for art would not jar aesthetic sensibilities.

His choice of objects that combine the practical and the aesthetic, such as a piece of old china or a sundial, reflects his view of the imagination as a creative faculty that fuses art and reality in a single consciousness. In the best of Lamb's essays imagination and understanding are not antagonistic faculties but complementary modes of experience.

Lamb's art is successful not because it shares elements with the works of his contemporaries, but because it is the careful creation of a true genius. It is an art that balances all the faculties—memory, feeling, understanding, and imagination.

# A SELECTED BIBLIOGRAPHY

## PRIMARY SOURCES

Lamb, Charles. *The Letters of Charles Lamb: To Which Are Added Those of His Sister Mary,* ed. E. V. Lucas. 3 vols. London: J. M. Dent; Methuen, 1935.

——————. *The Works of Charles and Mary Lamb,* ed. E. V. Lucas. 7 vols. London: Methuen, 1903-05.

## SECONDARY SOURCES

Abercrombie, Lascelles. *Romanticism.* New York: Barnes and Noble, 1963.

*The Art of Victorian Prose,* ed. George Levine and William Madden. London: Oxford Univ. Press, 1968.

Barnett, George L. *Charles Lamb: The Evolution of Elia.* Bloomington, Ind.: Indiana Univ. Press, 1964.

Bauer, Josephine. *The London Magazine.* Copenhagen: Rosenkilde and Bagger, 1953.

Bernbaum, Ernest. *Guide Through the Romantic Movement.* 2nd ed. New York: Ronald Press, 1949.

Blunden, Edmund. *Charles Lamb and His Contemporaries.* Hamden: Archon Books, 1967.

————. *Leigh Hunt's "Examiner" Examined.* London: Cobden-Sanderson, 1928.

*Charles Lamb: His Life Recorded by His Contemporaries,* compiled by Edmund Blunden. London: L. & Virginia Woolf, 1934.

Cornwall, Barry [B. W. Procter]. *Charles Lamb: A Memoir.* London: Edward Moxon, 1866.

Crawford, Thomas. *The Edinburgh Review and Romantic Poetry.* Auckland University College Bulletin, Ser. VIII, No. 47. Auckland, 1955.

De Quincey, Thomas. *The Works of Thomas De Quincey,* ed. David Masson. 14 vols. London: A. & C. Black, 1889-90.

Derocquigny, Jules. *Charles Lamb: Sa Vie et Ses Oeuvres.* Lille: L'Université, 1904.

Haven, Richard. "The Romantic Art of Charles Lamb," *ELH,* 30 (1963), 137-146.

Jack, Ian. *English Literature 1815-1832,* Vol. X of the *Oxford History of English Literature.* Ed. F. P. Wilson and Bonamy Dobreé. Oxford: Clarendon Press, 1963.

Johnson, Edith Christina. *Lamb Always Elia.* London: Methuen, 1935.

Keats, John. *The Letters of John Keats 1814-1821,* ed. Hyder E. Rollins. 2 vols. Cambridge, Mass.: Harvard Univ. Press, 1958.

————. *The Poetical Works of John Keats,* ed. H. W. Garrod. London: Oxford Univ. Press, 1956.

Klingopulos, G. G. "The Spirit of the Age in Prose", *From Blake to Byron,* Vol. V of *The Pelican Guide to English Literature.* Ed. Boris Ford. Harmondsworth: Penguin Books, 1957.

Van Kranendonk, A. G. "Notes on the Style of the Essays of Elia," *ES,* 14 (1932), 1-10.

Law, Marie Hamilton. *The English Familiar Essay in the Early Nineteenth Century.* New York: Russell & Russell, 1965.

Lucas, E. V. *The Life of Charles Lamb.* 5th ed. rev. 2 vols. London: Methuen, 1921.

MacDonald, W. L. "Charles Lamb, the Greatest of the Essayists," *PMLA,* 24 (1917), 547-572.

May, J. Lewis. *Charles Lamb: A Study.* London: Geoffrey Bles, 1934.

Morley, F. V. *Lamb before Elia.* London: Jonathan Cape, 1932.

Mulcahy, Daniel J. "Charles Lamb: The Antithetical Manner and the Two Planes," *SEL*, 3 (1963), 517-542.

Pater, Walter. "Charles Lamb," *Appreciations*. London: Macmillan, 1918, pp. 105-123.

Patterson, Charles I. "Charles Lamb's Insight into the Nature of the Novel," *PMLA*, 67 (1952), 375-382.

Praz, Mario. "The Letters of Charles Lamb or Religio Burgensis," *ES*, 18 (1936), 17-23.

Reiman, Donald H. "Thematic Unity in Lamb's Familiar Essays," *JEGP*, 64 (1965), 470-478.

Roberts, R. Ellis. "Charles Lamb," *Essays by Divers Hands*, Ser. III, No. 8. Ed. W. B. Maxwell, London: Oxford Univ. Press, 1934.

*Romanticism: Points of View*. Ed. Robert F. Gleckner and Gerald E. Enscoe. Englewood Cliffs, N. J.: Prentice-Hall, 1962.

Shelley, Percy Bysshe. *Complete Works* (Julian ed.), ed. Roger Ingpen and W. E. Peck. 10 vols. New York: Scribners, 1926-30.

Swinburne, Algernon Charles. "Charles Lamb and George Wither," *Miscellanies*. London: Chatto & Windus, 1886, pp. 157-200.

Tave, Stuart M. *The Amiable Humorist*. Chicago: University of Chicago Press, 1960.

—————. "Charles Lamb: Criticism," *The English Romantic Poets and Essayists: A Review of Research and Criticism*. Ed. Carolyn W. Houtchens and L. H. Houtchens. rev. ed. New York: New York Univ. Press, 1966, pp. 58-74.

Talfourd, Thomas Noon. *Final Memorials of Charles Lamb*. London: Edward Moxon, 1850.

Thompson, Denys. "Our Debt to Lamb," *Determinations*. Ed. F. R. Leavis. London: Chatto & Windus, 1934, pp. 199-217.

Tillotson, Geoffrey. "The Historical Importance of Certain 'Essays of Elia,'" *Some British Romantics*. Ed. James V. Logan, John E. Jordan, and Northrop Frye. Columbus: Ohio State Univ. Press, 1966, pp. 89-116.

Tillyard, E. M. W., ed. *Lamb's Criticism*. Cambridge, Eng.: The University Press, 1923.

Ward, William S. "Periodical Literature," *Some British Romantics*. Ed. James V. Logan, John E. Jordan, and Northrop Frye. Columbus: Ohio State Univ. Press, 1966, pp. 295-331.

Webb, Allie. "Charles Lamb's Use of the Character," *SQ*, (1963), 273-284.

Whitmore, Charles E. "The Field of the Essays," *PMLA*, 36 (1921), 551-564.

Williamson, George. "The Equation of the Essay," *SR*, 35 (1927), 73-77.

Wordsworth, William. *The Letters of William and Dorothy Wordsworths: The Middle Years*, ed. Ernest de Selincourt. 2 vols. Oxford: Clarendon Press, 1937.

——————. *The Poetical Works of William Wordsworth*, ed. Ernest de Selincourt and Helen Darbishire. rev. ed. 5 vols. Oxford: Clarendon Press, 1952-59.

——————. *The Prelude*, ed. Ernest de Selincourt. Oxford: Clarendon Press, 1926.

——————. *The Prose Works of William Wordsworth*, ed. Alexander B. Grosart. 3 vols. London: Edward Moxon, 1876.

Yeats, W. B. *The Collected Poems of W. B. Yeats*. New York: Macmillan, 1956.

# INDEX

141